just RISE UP!

A CALL TO
MAKE JESUS FAMOUS

SARAH FRANCIS MARTIN

THOMAS NELSON
Since 1798

NASHVILLE DALLAS MEXICO CITY RIO DE JANEIRO

Published in Nashville, Tennessee, by Thomas Nelson. Thomas Nelson is a trademark of HarperCollins Christian Publishing.

Page design and layout: Crosslin Creative

Thomas Nelson, Inc., titles may be purchased in bulk for educational, business, fund-raising, or sales promotional use. For information, please e-mail *SpecialMarkets@ThomasNelson.com*.

* Note: Italics in quotations from The Voice are used to "indicate words not directly tied to the dynamic translation of the original language" but that "bring out the nuance of the original, assist in completing ideas, and . . . provide readers with information that would have been obvious to the original audience" (The Voice, preface). Emphasis in quotations from The Voice is indicated with the use of boldface type.

9781401680152

Printed in the United States of America

14 15 16 17 18 [RRD] 6 5 4 3 2 1

To Greg and Grayson: thank you for coming alongside me.
May our family always reflect the fame of our King Jesus.
To my family at 2030 Grace Church: this book
was inspired by your servant love, bold faith and
desire to do life differently. Keep rising up!

Contents

Introduction

RISE UP!

Over the past year the Lord has laid a phrase on my heart that I just can't wrap my mind around, and I can't get it out of my head: RISE UP! I've wrestled with God over what this means: the implications, the life change required, the boldness called for when we make the decision to circle our entire existence around the fame of Jesus. All these things can be quite daunting at first consideration. But, if you are up for the challenge, join me in a journey where we will together seek out how God desires of us to live differently and even make tough choices as we do just that—all to make Jesus famous.

"Wait," you may say. "Isn't Jesus already famous in this world?" Oh, yes He is! But my question to you . . . is Jesus famous in your life? Do you seek Him out and worship Him in every twist and turn? Do you stand up—or RISE UP!—for His fame, to make His name known rather than your own? Do you go about even your day-to-day activities with a continual connection to His Spirit, thus allowing Jesus a place in your thoughts and emotions—even your frustrations?

As I interact with women from all over the country (and all over the world!), I feel this itch to be part of a movement. I see an underlying desire of women to make their lives count. I sense some complacency coupled with the desire to overcome that apathy—yet they just don't know how to go about it. Some of us are stuck between the motivation to seek after our own agenda and the innate and God-given desire to live for Him above all. It would be easy to live for ourselves, but we would again find ourselves back on the couch of complacency because an apathetic life lacks fulfillment and excitement. Rather, when we make the bold decision to make Jesus famous, we step into a kingdom reality where God directs us toward ever-heart-satisfying actions of worship, prayer and service of others. As I explore this concept of RISE UP! with my friends and readers, I love to hear how God is moving in this generation. We don't just desire to make our personal mark on the world. No, we know that even though our culture says, "Me! Me! See ME!" there is a bigger picture to capture, a bigger plan that goes well beyond ourselves, our own little world.

This movement spurs us toward lives of praise with kingdom perspective and humble hearts as we dream God's dreams and influence others to RISE UP! alongside us.

I am sensitive to the fact that what this book asks of you might very well freak you out and tempt you to shut it and shelve it. You may even be tempted to give this book away to someone else, someone who you believe is more equipped for a lifestyle of making Jesus famous; someone who hasn't disappointed Jesus in the past or made a royal mess of what He has given her. Please know this was my initial temptation. Then it struck me.

We can take hold of the courage and the authority to RISE UP only because Jesus did first. He made the divine choice to take on our sins at the cross of Calvary, and He rose and defeated death three days later. The door is now wide-open for us to fulfill this God-given desire to worship and make much of Jesus and thus spill our worship into every square inch of our life. The itch that nags at our hearts and minds to make our lives count for something is fulfilled when we live in the reality that there is victory over struggles, sin, discouragement, fear, and doubt because Jesus rose FIRST. He paved the way for us to journey through life with boldness, even if the unknown and the perceptions of the world around us tempt us to back off. Jesus paved the way for us to love God with all that we have and in turn, love others just the same. The act of rising up will reflect a heart that is ever grateful for God's continual forgiveness and desire to live in that freedom.

Let's tackle who this book is not for. *Just RISE UP!* is not for those of us who have it all together and live a perfect faith. It is not for those who already have the Bible figured out to the letter. If you are a woman who loves Jesus (even if you've only known Him for five minutes) and craves something bigger than yourself, then *Just RISE UP!* is for you. If you need a breakthrough in faith, *Just RISE UP!* is for you. And if you think it's thrilling (maybe even a bit frightening) to contemplate a big, bold belief in the King of kings, then once again, *Just RISE UP!* is for you.

But before we move on, I want to give you a peek into a recent conversation I had with my friend. Catie is in the process of navigating her career and recent location changes while growing in her love for Jesus. I wanted to get her opinion about our topic of rising up, so I pitched her a question.

SARAH Catie, do you get excited at the thought of being part of a movement of women who see the "bigger picture" and desire to do life differently than their peers to make Jesus famous?

CATIE In complete honesty, my initial reaction to "a generation rising up" and being a part of that scares me. I don't think it's because of the sort of negative connotation that goes with people "rising up" against something, but I do think it is because it is going so much against the grain of our society. I have always had a relationship with God and had faith, but I will be the first to admit it has been very weak at times. In the past I have been the person to roll my eyes at someone who does the "Jesus talk" and proclaims everything great He has done or is doing in her life. To me it all appears fake, even if that person was being sincere and genuine. I also think part of this is due to, unfortunately, the number of Christians I have met who speak this way but do not truly live in this way or as the Word directs. I understand we all make mistakes, and it is a lifelong process, but I'm talking about the people who seem all talk and no action.

Do you agree with what Catie is getting at here? Her initial reservation toward our RISE UP! conversation is understandable, as we have all either refrained from walking our talk or have encountered those whom we'd call hypocrites. It is almost as if this fear of not living up to what we proclaim locks us in a holding pattern (remember the couch of complacency?) so that we do nothing at all and our faith stands bland and mundane.

Catie and I continued the conversation about the importance of authenticity in today's world. She brought up valid reasons for not yet boldly vocalizing her faith to her family, peers, and people she encounters throughout the day, for fear of being that "Jesus talk" girl with no substance behind her words. Have you personally felt too intimidated to go against the grain? It can be daunting to contemplate a life and faith in which we might very well come under scrutiny. The good news: we are really only accountable to the Lord. As long as we live for Him, even in our mistakes and sin, His approval is all that really matters. No one else's.

We will address these valid fears and reservations in the following pages by digging into the Bible. There are plenty of examples of biblical men and women who stalled out with fear at the thought of rising up. God still used them in His grand plan. He wants to do the same with us. He is just waiting for us to seek Him with our whole hearts and to set ourselves apart and live out our faith. He is waiting for us to RISE UP!

When beginning work on this manuscript sitting at my favorite coffee shop, with my hot English breakfast tea, I accidentally typed RISE UP! as "RiSE UP!" Do you see that? The letter "i" is in lowercase. This served to remind me that this life decision is not about self. I need that reminder daily as I decide to make Jesus famous in my interaction with my girlfriends, to speak in a manner that encourages others rather than tears them down. I must choose to put aside my ego. Rising up means we get ourselves out of the way and live in a countercultural manner. It will not always be easy. It will not always be fun, either. To RISE UP! will cost much. But let me assure you that the benefits abound. Friends, our Jesus is worth it.

As we start our conversation together, let us prayerfully ask these questions:

What would happen if we chose to . . .

RISE UP! with integrity at our jobs and work as if our boss were Jesus?

RISE UP! and place Jesus at the center of every room in our household?

RISE UP! with our money and give until it hurts?

RISE UP! with our relationships and love even when that love isn't returned?

RISE UP! with our words and speak the fame and glory of Jesus even if people think we are weird?

RISE UP! with our actions and follow the Holy Spirit's leading—even if that leading takes us to uncomfortable places?

Let this movement of our lives—of our souls—not be just about words and motivational phrases that look nice on paper. Let us actually step up our faith and change our lives in real and practical ways.

Will you open your Bible to the book of Psalms? Our home base for this conversation will be Psalm 145. Take a look at four verses that have captured my imagination. I envision sparks all across the world that RISE UP! and live out the fame and glory of our King—women who love the Lord with all their hearts, minds, and souls, and desire to influence others to do the same.

You are one of those sparks. Don't let your spark go dormant with complacency. Don't let it die because of fear or uncertainty.

RISE UP!

> One generation *after another* will celebrate Your great works;
> they will pass on the story of Your powerful acts to their children.
> Your majesty and glorious splendor *have captivated me;*
> I will meditate on Your wonders, *sing songs of Your worth.*
> We confess—there is *nothing greater than You, God,* nothing mightier than Your awesome works.
> I will tell of *Your greatness as long as I have breath.*
> (Ps. 145:4–6)

Jesus said on Palm Sunday that the rocks would cry out if His people wouldn't praise Him (Luke 19:40). Oh, how I don't want to leave it up to the rocks! Let's not miss out on the pleasure of rising up, praising Him out loud, and living out our lives reflecting the greatness, mercy, joy, and majesty of Jesus.

Some Logistics of Our RISE UP! Conversation . . .

Before we dive into chapter 1, let me explain in just a few words how this book is set up. It is my hope that *Just RISE UP!* will be a catalyst toward meaningful conversations between you and the Lord. Each chapter is divided into five parts, each with its own journaling prompts. You are welcome to read the chapter through in one sitting or do it in five days, one segment at a time. One thing, though: promise me you will actually keep a journal as you read this book. Promise? Okay, great! These sections are really where the rubber meets the road in our journey to RISE UP! It is so important for our personal spiritual growth that we take time to think it through, talk to God, and hear from Him through the Bible. The journal sections will help facilitate that. If you find that writing and journaling is not your thing, know that these sections don't have to be perfectly eloquent prose. Look at these journal prompts as a tool to pinpoint your thoughts and communication with Jesus. There is something to be said for using multiple senses when interacting with the Bible. When we engage our minds and our sense of touch (by using a pen and paper), we become more focused and less likely to tune out or get distracted. Trust me; it will be powerful. The journal doesn't have to be anything fancy, but rather, a space for you and Jesus.

At the beginning of each chapter I've included pieces of conversation between me and my friends surrounding our various topics regarding the movement to RISE UP! As I wrote *Just RISE UP!* I reached out to a handful of girlfriends I knew I could trust to share their real and raw thoughts surrounding our concept of making Jesus famous. I will share snippets of these conversations as I invite you into an overall conversation throughout the following pages. The bottom line is that we are in this together. If you have an itch to do life differently, to make bold choices towards the fame of Jesus, join me in this conversation.

The final section of each chapter is titled "Do Life Differently." This has become a personal catchphrase of mine that I hope you will adopt for yourself as well. As we move through our conversation, I hope to encourage you, maybe even challenge you, to make changes in your life that reflect your heart to RISE UP! These changes may be tough, but blessings are to behold when we walk in obedience and strive to please the Lord with our day-to-day actions and thoughts. I've worked hard to make these "Do Life Differently" prompts very applicable to real-life, and I pray you will consider them and apply them.

One more thing: at the end of the book you will find a short and simple conversation starter should you decide to gather some friends to RISE UP and go through the book together. Be sure to check it out.

So, are you ready to begin? I am! Let's jump right in. Grab a journal and pen. Today, will you join me in some thoughtful journaling through the idea of rising up?

First, find some quiet space in your brain to search out why you desire to rise up—if you desire to RISE UP! Though everything in me wants to jump feet-first into this, I know I must come at it with a heart prepared for major change and transformation. I invite you to take some time and journal through the following questions. Let these words be a prayer and a declaration to God that you are ready and willing to RISE UP!

- If I have the desire to RISE UP! what is my true motivation?
- In what areas of my life should I not rely on myself and, instead, trust God?

Now pray through these areas, and confess to the Lord why you've left Him out.

Next, list ways that you need God to move in your life and in the world around you.

Now tell Him how much you trust Him to do great things, in His way, in your life and in your world.

Finally, name several ways that the Lord is already moving around you, where you can see His hand at work on the inside or in the circumstances of your life.[1]

CHAPTER ONE

A Life of Praise

As I mentioned in the introduction, Psalm 145 will be our home base for this journey. This psalm is titled "A song of praise by David," and it is my hope that by the end of this book we each will live a life that reflects daily praise of Jesus. Our lips will utter words that point straight to Him; our minds will be consumed with thoughts of how great He is. The way we live should reflect hearts that know He is worthy. Living a life of praise is a daily choice, and this is where our call to RISE UP! and make Jesus famous comes into play. Sometimes we just don't feel like it. Twists and turns take us down roads where we must decide: will I wallow in self-doubt or pity? Or will I choose to praise Jesus anyway?

This concept of living a life of praise prepares us nicely as we RISE UP! For when, we turn our focus and adoration outward and upward toward Jesus, we step out of ourselves and our self-focused perspective. We welcome His path for our lives when we step out of the present pain or frustration and into even the unknown road ahead with a new level of trust. This is what praise does; it clears out our preconceived notions and puts us in a place where we recognize that God is good and He is powerful. Our hearts pump with passion because He made us for worship. Our spirits sing with joy because the Author of joy blesses those who call upon His name in praise. Our minds de-clutter of stress and worry when we get over ourselves and make much of Jesus.

What matters at the end of the day is not what actually happened to lead to that crossroads. No, what matters most is the choice to praise

God or not to praise Him. It takes faith to RISE UP! and live a life of praise. Choice by choice we decide to lift His name high in our life dramas, and our hearts transform into hearts full of trust and reverence for the almighty God.

Reverence is key. This does not come naturally to most of us. Our society and our human nature lean toward the irreverent. May we recognize the call deep down in our hearts, which God planted Himself, to revere and worship Him alone. May we live out each day with lips, thoughts, and actions full of praise.

Here is a small snippet of a conversation I had with my friend Lou on this very topic:

SARAH Lou. Now that you've had a chance to read Psalm 145:1–9, where David wrote so beautifully about living a life of praise, what do you think about this concept?

LOU I love the concept of living a life of praise, although I do struggle with it a lot. I don't know if that's because in my current life situation, I feel I am maybe not living to my full potential and so I become frustrated and bogged down with the "what could be's" instead of enjoying my life that God has blessed me with and giving Him the glory that He deserves. As a Christian, living a life of praise is something that should come naturally, but again, it doesn't!

I agree wholeheartedly with Lou. Living a life of praise doesn't always come naturally. That's why we need to soak in the Word and take David's example in Psalm 145. And the more we do it—praise the Lord no matter what—the more natural it becomes to us. When we decide to RISE UP! and not allow people or circumstances to interrupt our life of praise, we actually make an impression on those in our lives.

As our conversation progressed, Lou went on to explain that she sometimes feels it is easier to sit in front of the TV or Facebook, or the Internet in general, than spend time with the Lord. She added, "I am easily agitated when I am not spending time in the Bible or in prayer, yet when my focus is on God, He very clearly gives me the patience and compassion to not get angry but just to let it go. It all boils down to your heart's motives and consciously keeping Jesus at the center of your life. Living a life of praise lifts my spirit to be able to look beyond the mundane in life, like being stuck in a job that I'm not entirely satisfied with, and enables me to work and live with the thought that God is involved in everything in my life. This includes my job. So how does that play out in my life? It means that I am able to love people freely, again looking beyond a face and knowing that they, too, are created in the image of God."

When we turn our focus and adoration outward and upward toward Jesus, we step out of ourselves and our self-focused perspective.

Like, Lou, I often allow my circumstances or certain people around me to disrupt my attitude of praise. The ideal scenario is that I turn to scriptures such as Psalm 145 to remind me what a life of praise looks like regardless of life drama. The more we immerse ourselves in the pure truth of the Bible, the more naturally we make the minute-by-minute choice to worship Jesus in every mountain and valley in life. Take some time with the following journal questions as we begin digging into Psalm 145. As we develop our theme throughout this book, it is my hope that you will encounter Jesus in your own private conversations with God almighty. He is ready and waiting. Grab your pen and your journal, and don't hesitate to write your real and raw feelings in your journal.

Journal 1
A LIFE OF PRAISE

In your own Bible read through Psalm 145. We will be reading this scripture over and over throughout our time together. The more we soak in this Psalm, the more we will reflect our own lives of praise!

Use any or all of these journal prompts to help you process everything you've read.

- ☐ What are your thoughts on the concept of "living a life of praise"? How do you define a life of praise?
- ☐ What are some of your own regular distractions that keep you disconnected from the Lord and draw you away from a life of praise?
- ☐ As mentioned earlier, reverence for our King is the key to living a life of praise. Look up the word "reverence." What does this definition make you think about regarding living a life of praise in reverence of Jesus?

RISE UP! in Prayer

Use these prayer prompts to work through via prayer what you've learned so far about living a life of praise. If you like, you can write your prayers out in your journal.

- King Jesus, forgive me when I allow life to distract me from a life of praise by . . .
- Lord, open my heart to see You in all that I do so I will live a life of praise by . . .

A Language of Praise

I'm ashamed to confess that I once had a serious problem with my language. I used to curse and swear with the best of them. Four-letter words would roll off my tongue with ease, and not only when I was angry and couldn't control my temper. Foul language was just part of my speech, and I thought I was really cool dropping crude words constantly. I cringe now at the thought of my profanity, which simply reflected the ugly junk in my heart. What did my language portray to others? A frustrated heart. A heart not at peace with her present life situation, and whose only way to express discontent was to throw out ugly language.

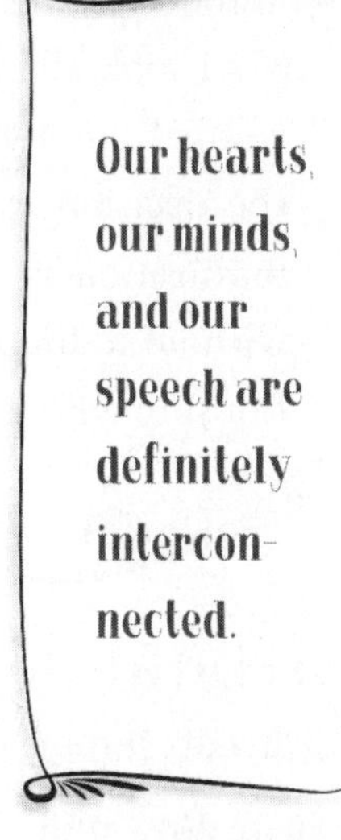
Our hearts, our minds, and our speech are definitely intercon-nected.

Our hearts, our minds, and our speech are definitely interconnected. In the past, my mind wasn't focused on Jesus and His goodness. Thus, my words did not bring goodness to the world around me. Years later, I continually find ways to better reflect a life of praise, one that worships Jesus with my mind, my heart, and my mouth.

There is always something to improve on; I am a work in progress. This realization brought me to a new mouth-tweak, if you will. In time, though I no longer spoke the f-word or the sh-word, OMGs were a regular part of my vernacular. I'm not just talking about a text shortcut. "Oh, my God!" and "Oh, God!" spilled out of my mouth as sentence exclamations. During this time I had a true desire to fully live out my faith, and I knew deep in my heart that OMGs are irreverent. In the Bible it is called "tak[ing] the name of the Lord . . . in vain" (Ex. 20:7 NKJV). I was using the holy name GOD in a light manner—tossing it around uselessly. If I really knew the power of His name, I wouldn't "OMG" unless my heart was truly calling out in praise or in prayer.

It took quite a while to undo this OMG habit of mine. The more I took time to praise the Lord and read praise-filled scripture, like the

Psalms, the more I protected the name of the Lord in my heart and used it only when singing His name or calling out in prayer. It is crucial to evaluate our language when we desire to live a life of praise. No one likes a hypocrite. Think about what kind of example we set if we proclaim the name of Jesus in one sentence, attempting to make Him famous, and then, in the next sentence, we throw out an irreverent "Oh, my God!" or crude and demeaning words.

I took all of this into account when I decided to kill OMG and curse words from my vocabulary. Habits are hard to get rid of. What solidified the decision was when I truly grasped the idea that my outward communication is a reflection of what's in my heart. I knew I loved Jesus, without a doubt. This was one of those "go deeper" moments in my relationship with the Lord as I recognized how imperative it is to live a life of praise from the inside out. Inside, my heart and mind were transforming such that there was no way I could continue to allow my words to stand irreverent of my Jesus. It was a natural progression at this point, with my speech, to reflect this revived reverence for Him. Some habits aren't so easy to flip the switch and get rid of. But knowing that what I speak should reflect what I believe, I literally flipped the switch one day and eliminated the obscenity.

The fact is that life gets tough some days, and living a life of praise doesn't mean that we refrain from talking about the not-so-great issues in our lives.

In the quest to RISE UP! what should we speak?

We don't want to be like those who talk constantly, with sugarcoated phrases, about how good life is. That is not realistic. The fact is that life gets tough some days, and living a life of praise doesn't mean that we refrain from talking about the not-so-great issues in our lives. There is great freedom in a life of praise that says . . .

- "Lord, I will praise You today even though I can't pay these bills, for You have shown up in the past, and I trust that you will provide in this time of need."
- "Lord, I will praise You today when I'm frustrated beyond belief with work. You alone provide the contentment and peace I need to push through and perform my job with excellence."

"Every good gift bestowed, every perfect gift received comes to *us* from above, courtesy of the Father of lights. He *is consistent*. He won't change His mind or play tricks in the shadows." (James 1:17)

On the flip side, when the good days roll around, a life full of praise does not forget to give Jesus the credit. It's all too easy to keep truckin' on the good days and neglect to praise the One from whom all good things come. For when "every good [and] . . . perfect gift" that "comes to us from above" graces our lives (James 1:17), what better time to put aside our egos and lift up the name of Jesus? May our lips be full of praise.

- "Lord, You have created this beautiful, sunny day. I thank You for the opportunity to enjoy fresh air and time in the sun today with my family at the park."
- "Lord, I did well on that exam! Thank You for giving me the strength to study last night and for helping me stay calm while taking the test."

Take a look at what Philippians has to say about the day when everyone in heaven and on earth will bow down and use their tongues to proclaim the name of God.

> So God raised Him up to the highest place and gave Him the name above all. So when His name is called, every knee will bow, in heaven,

> on earth, and below. And every tongue will confess "Jesus, the Anointed One, is Lord," to the glory of God our Father! (Phil. 2:9–11)

This verse tells us that every tongue will confess Jesus' name as Lord, not just those who are professed Christians. On that day, the entire creation will cry out and praise His name, with bended knee, in humility and reverence. But why should we, women who desire to RISE UP! and make Jesus famous in our lives right here and right now, wait until that fateful day? What is keeping each of us from living a life full of praise daily? What is stopping us from saying, "Jesus! You are my King and the one true God. I give you glory and honor today"?

Let's solidify this concept of a language of praise as we dig into Psalm 145:1–3. Join me in the Bible study and journal questions in the next few pages to take up David's example in his "song of praise."

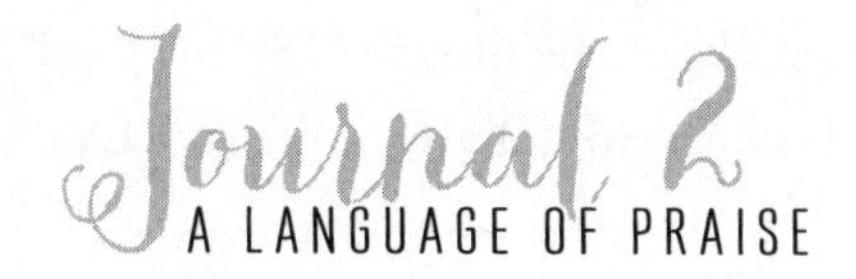

Journal 2: A LANGUAGE OF PRAISE

A Praise of David

I will extol You, my God, O King;
And I will bless Your name forever and ever.
Every day I will bless You,
And I will praise Your name forever and ever.
Great is the LORD, and greatly to be praised;
And His greatness is unsearchable.

One generation shall praise Your works to another,
And shall declare Your mighty acts.
I will meditate on the glorious splendor of Your majesty,
And on Your wondrous works.
Men shall speak of the might of Your awesome acts,
And I will declare Your greatness.
They shall utter the memory of Your great goodness,
And shall sing of Your righteousness. (Ps. 145:1–7 NKJV)

In this song of praise written by David, we are invited to join him in praising God's majesty and love. This psalm starts us out in a very personal manner of praise. Notice how intimate David made his praise.

I will extol You, my God, O King.

☐ Do you see the importance of claiming God as "my God"? Think about your present manner of praising God. Do you make it personal, as David did? If not, why? Is there something keeping you from living a life of praise such that you claim God as yours?

- ☐ How does our conversation about the phrase "Oh, my God!" change your point of view concerning living a life of REVERENT praise?
- ☐ Reread verses 1–7 from Psalm 145. Notice how many times David wrote the phrase I will.
- ☐ Write the word that follows each "I will" (example: I will bless):
- ☐ Each "I will . . ." statement is a bold declaration toward a life of praise. Think about how you can live your life of praise with these bold declarations, and write it down. For instance, how can you declare God's greatness in your life today? Think of practical ways of living a life of praise.
- ☐ What challenges do you see in the concept of living a life of praise with the words you speak daily? (Look at my example, as I had to reexamine my use of "Oh, my God!" and trade it for bold declarations such as the "I will" statements.)

RISE UP! in Prayer

Take some time to finish this prayer prompt with your own words in your personal journal.

- Father, You are worthy of my praise because You are . . .
- Thank You for allowing me into Your presence so that I may experience Your glory. Help me to go out and live a life of praise with my words . . .

Thoughts of Praise

Do you ever lie in bed late at night, unable to sleep, because you've allowed your thoughts to take you down a dark path and get the better of you? Our minds have a way of twisting and turning reality until we only see puzzle pieces that will never fit together. In the darkness of a late night or the murkiness of a difficult life season, we have a continuous choice to make: will we allow our thoughts to lead us to false reality, or will we RISE UP!—even in our minds—and recognize God's truth? This takes a daily practice of setting our minds straight on Him as our ultimate reality.

A.W. Tozer said it perfectly: "You can see God from anywhere if your mind is set to love and obey Him."[1]

If we choose thoughts of praise, we are loving Him with our minds. This takes a commitment to "bless [His] name forever and ever" as Psalm 145:1 states (NKJV). To me, "forever and ever" encompasses the minute-by-minute of life, regardless of our stress, regardless of whether or not we feel like it. I am rising up and loving God with my mind if I overlook what I see in the here and now and look through the perspective that God is bigger than anything we are struggling with.

The other day I received a text from my friend Chelsey, who is in the thick of nursing school—tough classes with an obscene number of tests. I knew from previous conversations that Chelsey has been in over her head, struggling with the pressure of school and allowing that to affect her trust in God's goodness to provide exactly what she needs. Over and over again, I read her Facebook updates expressing the need for prayer—pleas, in fact. Because I know Chelsey so well, I knew these pleas indicated an underlying issue of doubt and fear. This was a drastic turn from her regular praise of Jesus just a few months ago. Chelsey allowed life's stress to dredge up old feelings of doubt and distrust that God will hold and keep her in her time of need.

> **His greatness doesn't depend on what we think of Him, but our faith is greatly increased when we dwell on and love Him with grand thoughts.**

Without downplaying her palpable anxiety (which we all experience), I encouraged Chelsey with these words in response to her pleading for prayer: "Girl. I totally hear you, and you know I'm praying. Do your best NOT to cling to the seemingly tangible stress, fear, and doubt. Sometimes faith seems less tangible and difficult to grasp. Keep reminding yourself how good your God is and how He has carried you through school over the last few months."

I wonder how many of us take minutes and hours in the day to dwell on how stressed we are, instead of dwelling on Jesus and loving Him with our thoughts. How often do we sit in a private (or not-so-private) pity party, consumed with how bad life is, and maybe even make it worse than it really is. When we rehearse over and over in our minds how tough life is, we are pushing out the truth, that God is bigger than anything that is weighing us down. Our brain energy is better spent on rehearsing this thought process:

> I will meditate on the glorious splendor of Your majesty,
> And on Your wondrous works. (Ps. 145:5 NKJV)

Investigate your heart and evaluate whether or not you truly believe in the greatness of your God. His greatness doesn't depend on what we think of Him, but our faith is greatly increased when we dwell on and love Him with grand thoughts. Our faith will not grow if we spend the day focused inward on our own troubles, but when we turn our focus toward God, we see the awesome ways God chooses to bless us. We can reach a new level of faith where we don't simply think about God and His majesty, but we also long to spread news of His goodness with our words. Thoughts coming from a changed heart translate into words of praise.

Seeing God's hand in our stressful times takes a measure of obedience on our part. Obeying God with our minds means we don't entertain thoughts that keep us bound in chains of sin, doubt, distrust, or self-loathing. Let us take to the cross the ugly parts of our hearts and minds that lead to ugly actions. Jesus died on the cross so we don't have to live in bondage to the dark parts of our minds. We must choose to exchange the darkness for the clarity and light of praise.

There is a fantastic passage in Acts 16 where Paul and Silas were in jail, bound with chains. These two men of God were innocent. They could have chosen to dwell on the injustice of their present circumstances and allowed their minds to stay in the darkness. Instead, they chose to obey God and praise Him regardless.

> *Picture this: It's midnight. In the darkness of their cell,* Paul and Silas—*after surviving the severe beating—aren't moaning and groaning;* they're praying and singing hymns to God. The prisoners *in adjoining cells are wide awake,* listening to them pray and sing. Suddenly the ground begins to shake, and the prison foundations begin to crack. You can hear the sound of jangling chains and the squeak of cell doors opening. Every prisoner realizes that his chains have come unfastened. (Acts 16:25–26)

With shouts of praise, your chains of doubt are broken!

With thoughts of His greatness and pleas for forgiveness, the chains of past and present sin are broken!

With exclamations of wonder at God's glory, chains binding you to ugly memories of pain are broken!

With bold declarations that you will RISE UP! and live a life of praise, chains are broken and you are free to experience the blessings that come with obedience.

Journal 3
THOUGHTS OF PRAISE

Spend a few minutes revisiting Psalm 145:5.

> Your majesty and glorious splendor *have captivated me;*
> I will meditate on Your wonders, *sing songs of Your worth.*

I invite you to meditate on God's wonders and His worth. This may come in the form of words of thanksgiving as you recount blessings for which you are grateful. Giving thanks serves to rearrange our thinking in the present and remind us of how God has worked in our lives in the past. Meditating and giving thanks remind us that regardless of our present circumstances, He is for us and not against us. (See Romans 8:31.)

- [ ] Write out whatever comes to mind as you meditate on His "majesty and glorious splendor." (If you are having a tough time with meditations of thanksgiving, write out a prayer asking God to bring things to mind for which you are grateful.)

In this chapter we have examined how our heart condition and actions are directly affected by our thoughts. Our thoughts then turn into words . . . for better or for worse.

- [ ] What do you see as the benefit of rising up and living a life of praise with your thoughts and words? How can this life of praise positively affect your life and the words you express?

RISE UP! in Prayer

Take some time to finish this prayer prompt with your own words in your personal journal.

- Father, forgive me for these things that keep me in bondage . . .
- I choose today to praise You with my thoughts. You are . . .
- Lord, show me how to RISE UP! as you break the chains and free me to live a life of praise . . .

Lifestyle of Praise

In order to RISE UP! and create a lifestyle of praise (with thoughts, words, and actions), we must live in constant pursuit of Christ. We must worship Him simply because He is ever so worthy and not for what we can "get out of it."

I find myself cringing whenever I talk to someone about his or her recent experience at church or at a Bible study and the person says, "Well, I really didn't get much out of it." I, too, have fallen victim to this type of thinking, but I realized that these thoughts came from being naive about my life purpose. Though the church experience is for our benefit (to learn from biblical teaching and to connect with others who love Jesus), it is also a divine opportunity to join in with the heavenly choir and corporately praise and honor God. It is not about you or me or what we "get out of it." No, we are called to a lifestyle that revolves around God's majesty.

What does a lifestyle of praise look like?

> lifestyle: A way of life or style of living that reflects the attitudes and values of a person or group[2]

Whether we like it or not, our lives will reflect our true "attitudes and values." We are called to authentic faith, a faith immersed in reverence and commitment and not what we can "get out of it." I believe this generation craves authenticity. When we watch television or flip through magazines, we see nothing but slick, photoshopped lives, which stand far from our own reality. We can easily turn and do the same through social media. How often do our Facebook status updates show what is really going on in our lives?

AUTHENTIC FAITH: REVERENCE AND COMMITMENT

I truly believe that people in this generation respect those who stand for something, who live differently because they believe in something—anything—greater than themselves. This goes back to the desire to make your "mark" on the world. We have the opportunity to make a meaningful and eternal mark when we model lives of praise, when we live an authentic faith, full of reverence and commitment to the King of kings. Our friends and family may not always understand just who it is we serve and why we place Him above all, but our authenticity in faith will catch their attention. Even those who say they are Christians but don't live out their faith will be challenged to examine what they believe or in whom they believe when they see us living differently for the sake of making Jesus famous. They may think we are weird. Weird is good! It means we are set apart from the pack . . . exactly what the Bible says we are supposed to be (2 Cor. 6:17).

Outward reverence for Christ comes into play when our lifestyle makes it obvious that we care more about His name being renowned in our lives than about what others think. Outward commitment to Christ is shown when we make difficult life decisions. When we boldly step out in faith to say no to things that displease Him and yes to things that bless His name, God is honored.

Our church experience is a divine opportunity to join in with the heavenly choir and corporately praise and honor God.

So far in this section we have discussed outward expressions of authentic faith full of reverence and commitment. But the root of this kind of lifestyle must come from inside. The condition of our hearts—full of reverence for His name and commitment to love and obey Him always—steers us to a long-lasting passion to live with boldness for the fame of Jesus. When we cultivate a lifestyle that praises God daily, a strong passion arises. This passion is a daily discipline and a choice that starts with our thoughts which affect our actions and outward expressions. I encourage you to soak in the following qualities of Christ in order to spark your passion as you daily pursue more of Jesus.

> Finally, brothers and sisters, fill your minds with *beauty and* truth. Meditate on whatever is honorable, whatever is right, whatever is pure, whatever is lovely, whatever is good, whatever is virtuous and praiseworthy. Keep to the script: whatever you learned and received and heard and saw in me—do it—and the God of peace will walk with you. (Phil. 4:8–9)

I love how this translation uses the wording "fill your minds" and "meditate on" It reminds us that God does not just say, "Don't think bad thoughts"; He gives us a positive alternative. When we meditate on what is beautiful and true, there is no room for sick and sinful thinking. All of the qualities in this passage come straight from who Jesus is. He is pure. He is good. He is praiseworthy. It is to our benefit to fill up with these same qualities and emulate Him. To be authentic is to be made in the same way as an original. Our "original" is Jesus. We live the most authentic lifestyle when we live the same way (both inside, in our hearts, and outside, through our actions) that Jesus did. How quickly that authenticity can wane and our passion can be quelled when we fill our minds with anything that is not blessed by God!

To be authentic is to be made in the same way as an original. Our "original" is Jesus.

Inward reverence and commitment go hand in hand with this as well. Inner reverence for Christ is shown when we dwell on Him above all else. He is more satisfying than anything money can buy, any romantic relationship, any love for a child, any job, any friendship, or any hobby. This level of commitment to Christ is shown when we deny ourselves pride, jealousy, or anger because they threaten obedience and joy.

Do you get fired up at the thought of a lifestyle of authentic faith and praise? I do. I said earlier that I envision women all over the world as sparks, lighting a fire and challenging others to RISE UP! along with them and make Jesus famous. The potential impact that we make has eternal effects. We want to make a mark on our world, but not one that points to our own achievements. Instead, we want to leave an impression on hearts that will point them to the goodness of Jesus. It starts with inward reverence and commitment, and then bold obedience to the call to RISE UP! with outward authenticity of faith.

How will you practice reverence and commitment as you RISE UP! and make Jesus famous?

Journal 4
A LIFESTYLE OF PRAISE

Take a look back at the definition of the word lifestyle. How would you personally define a lifestyle of praise?

Let's circle back to the first few verses of Psalm 145:

> I will lift my praise *above everything* to You, my God and King!
> I will *continually* bless Your name forever and always.
> *My praise will never cease—*
> I will praise You every day;
> I will lift up Your name forever.
> The Eternal is great and deserves endless praise;
> *His greatness knows no limit, recognizes no boundary.*
> No one can measure or comprehend His magnificence.
> (vv. 1–3)

These verses are full of statements of reverence and commitment. Be sure to take note of any phrases that speak of reverence for Jesus (example: "No one can measure").

- ☐ How would you express your own reverence for Jesus?
- ☐ Take note of the phrases that speak of commitment to Jesus (example: "I will continually"). How would you express your own commitment?
- ☐ What are your thoughts on the concept of outward and inward reverence and commitment?
- ☐ How can you start with inner reverence and commitment today? (Example: Commit to study the qualities of Christ listed in Philippians 4:8–9, or take time daily to sit in prayer with a reverent heart, praising God for His greatness.)

RISE UP! in Prayer

Take some time to finish this prayer prompt with your own words in your personal journal.

- Lord, forgive me when I don't show you reverence and commitment in these ways . . .
- Father God, You are worthy of my praise because . . .
- Lord, show me how I can commit to you in my heart and in my outward actions today . . .

RISE UP!
Do Life Differently

I am the type of writer who loves a good !!! or :) :) or even !?! to end my sentences. I like to express myself exuberantly!

The other night at church, our leader, Ryan, started an evening of prayer with a wild concept: what if we approached that night with an all-out expectation that God's presence would surround us as we sang in worship? We all closed our eyes and imagined that our prayer and worship would rip open an unseen element and that the actual kingdom of heaven would come down on that room. As the band played songs that led us in verses of praise for God's glory and goodness, an eruption of clapping, yelling, and praising raised the roof of the room and welcomed in the overwhelming presence and glory of the Lord.

What happened that night for me was an increased level of expectation of God's glory as we collectively praised and worshipped Him. We set our hearts in expectation that God would show up in His way—in His timing—and we praised Him for His faithfulness. Though we pursued God's presence as a group, that night showed me the importance of even a private pursuit of God. As we chase after God, He promises that He will be found (see Jeremiah 29:13–14). This pursuit must be coupled with a deeper level of trust and thanksgiving on the front end. For if we decide to do life differently, filling our thoughts and words with praise, and to seek after God's will and path for our lives, we must allow ourselves to trust Jesus for the outcome. Whatever God has for us and wherever He leads us, we must RISE UP! and praise Him with thankful hearts.

This is not to say that our trust in the Lord and our praise to Him are centered only on the emotions of worship. Rather, this newfound desire to live a life of praise is based on what we know is truth: that He is worthy of our pursuit. Some days, we just can't depend on the emotion of worship due to circumstances weighing heavy on our hearts. There are some seasons when we just don't want to exuberantly praise Him. When it comes down to it, as we make much of Jesus in our life, we do so even when our emotions don't match up to what we know is truth. These are times where we rely on God's truth, which tells us, "Come to Me; I'll give you rest for your soul" (see Matthew 11:28).

I want to have an attitude of praise that is not dependent on circumstances or emotions, but one that comes from deep inside and is rooted in God's Word. I want to join in with the generations past who declared God's goodness because He is the One who deserves my utmost renown. As we praise Him with our lifestyle, we make the name of Jesus famous.

> One generation *after another* will celebrate Your great works;
> they will pass on the story of Your powerful acts to their children.
> Your majesty and glorious splendor *have captivated me;*
> I will meditate on Your wonders, *sing songs of Your worth.*
> We confess—*there is nothing greater than You, God,* nothing mightier than Your awesome works.
> I will tell of Your greatness *as long as I have breath.*
> *The news of* Your rich goodness *is no secret—*
> Your people love to recall it
> and sing songs of *joy to celebrate* Your righteousness.
> (Ps. 145:4–7)

This doesn't mean we must go around all the time clapping and yelling about the Lord. (Those actions are great but not always appropriate.) But what it does mean is that even in tough life situations, our faith in Him is front and center, and we express how He is moving to those around us. By simply living with Christ front and center, we portray Him to those around us—in our families, at work, or even at school.

Get excited about your King, Jesus!!

If you've searched your heart while reading this and come up dry—no exclamation point—please hear me: ask for it. God is the Author and perfecter of our emotions. All we have to do is come to Him with an honest heart, open to Him, and He will give us the excitement for His glory that we might lack. He will fill in the gaps. He will give us reason for an exclamation point–type of attitude. Pray for eyes to see the ways He is moving in and around you. Ask Him to cultivate more than just emotion inside you. Ask God to stir your heart so you can't help but live your life with excitement for His presence.

Ask God to stir your heart so you can't help but live your life with excitement for His presence.

An "exclamation point" attitude then leads us to live out our faith with a life of praise.

This will require us to make some tough decisions as we choose God's fame over our own creature comforts, our own fame, our own grand plans. But in the end, the life of praise will result in that which is much more fulfilling and satisfying. We were created to glorify God with our lives, and until we are fulfilling this purpose, we will feel something lacking. This is where some people go astray, though. They take that innate feeling of a need for purpose and make it all about "finding" themselves. This ends in a shallow journey toward self-exploration rather than a journey of experiencing the fulfilling presence of the almighty King. May we all do life differently for the sake of living outside of ourselves and take part in a greater kingdom purpose.

Journal 5 DO LIFE DIFFERENTLY

We will end each chapter with the topic "Do Life Differently." It is my hope that you will dig deep and journal through real and practical ways to apply the concepts of each chapter. Take some time to work through these questions, and then commit to actually following through. Grab your journal and put pen to paper with your thoughts toward doing life differently.

- ☐ Let's first explore your definition of "doing life differently" as you live a life of praise to make Christ famous. What does this mean to you at this stage of your life?
- ☐ Have you ever made a positive change in your life but realized you had the wrong motivations? Maybe selfish ones? Maybe prideful ones? Anything that didn't have the fame of Jesus as the priority? How did that turn out?
- ☐ How might you do life differently with the words you choose?
- ☐ How might you do life differently with your thoughts?
- ☐ How can you do life differently with your lifestyle?
- ☐ What difference does your heart attitude make in the effectiveness of your life changes?

Take some time to think and pray through a bold declaration you want to make for your life TODAY. We can be bold because we are standing on a foundation of faith that relies on the greatness of God, not the greatness of ourselves. Example: "Today I DECLARE that I will evaluate the words I use and eliminate words that do nothing to make Jesus famous in my life."

What actions can you take to live out that bold declaration?

RISE UP! in Prayer

Finish this prayer prompt with your own words in your personal journal.

- Lord, mold my heart to expect Your glory. I am thankful in advance in these ways . . .
- Father, give me the courage to make these bold declarations . . .

Notes

Notes

CHAPTER TWO

BE **Kingdom** MINDED

I hope by now that you have actually taken time to find real, tangible ways to live a life of praise. The concept we are diving into next will help you see the importance and benefits of praising the Lord with every area of life.

Kingdom Perspective

In this chapter we are going to look at how to develop our focus upward and outward toward things that are eternal—things that have lasting significance. We will also talk about ways to actually live out a kingdom perspective. I would hate for us to take our precious time in conversation about it, yet never actually implement this perspective in our lives.

Over the years I've developed a ministry catchphrase that serves as a personal reminder and a public declaration of where my perspective stands day by day

LIVING OUT! the kingship of Christ.

We can use this phrase as a way to prepare us in our conversation about a kingdom perspective and ultimately about the kingdom of God. We see throughout the Bible a number of phrases that come together synonymously to capture the meaning of God's kingdom: "kingdom of heaven," "kingdom of Christ," "kingdom of the Lord." (See, for example, Matthew 3:2; 6:33; 18:18.) These phrases all refer to the eternal power and authority of God as our Lord and Creator. The kingdom of God is . . . So just what is the kingdom of God, really?

- The kingdom of God is the reign of Christ—which seems odd and upside down to the world, yet gloriously logical in God's kingdom.

  Every kingdom has a king. But where most kings rule out of self-elevation and pride, our King came and served us first. He set the bar for us to follow as servants, and we can do that with the utmost dignity because we live and serve the King who defines the words good, beautiful, mighty, merciful, and grace.

  Adopt the mindset of Jesus the Anointed. He came not to be served, but to serve. Live with His attitude in your hearts. Remember:

  Though He was in the form of God,
  He chose not to cling to equality with God;
  But He poured Himself out *to fill a vessel brand new;*
  a servant in form
  and a man indeed.
  The very likeness of humanity,
  He humbled Himself,
  obedient to death—
  a merciless death on the cross!
  So God raised Him up to the highest place
  and gave Him the name above all.
  So when His name is called,
  every knee will bow,
  in heaven, on earth, and below.
  And every tongue will confess
  "Jesus, the Anointed One, is Lord,"
  to the glory of God our Father!
  (Phil. 2:5–11)

- The kingdom of God is a present reality—God created the universe and actively interacts with His creation.

> It was by Him that everything was created: the heavens, the earth, all things within and upon them, all things seen and unseen, thrones and dominions, *spiritual* powers and authorities. Every detail was crafted through His design, by *His own hands,* and for His purposes. (Col. 1:16)

We choose to participate in the kingdom when we decide to make Jesus and His Word the center of our lives, our utmost reality. The kingdom of God will continue on with or without us, but oh, what we will miss out on if we only watch from afar. By worshipping God as our Creator and taking part in His kingdom activities, we have the privilege of allowing God to use us for His ultimate purposes, as in Colossians 1:16.

We choose to participate in the kingdom when we decide to make Jesus and His Word the center of our lives, our utmost reality.

God's kingdom is here and now. His authority over all is undeniable, though many choose to live blind to it and to fight against His power. Knowing that He reigns over all the universe, we evaluate our priorities and where our loyalties stand, and our perspective adjusts.

- The kingdom of God is a future reality. As we live in the present with a kingdom perspective, the notion that Christ's kingdom shall have "no end" (Isa. 9:7 NKJV) serves as pure encouragement to look forward to our eternal communion and relationship with God. This concept should make us stop everyday and consider what is eternal rather than focusing on the things of this earth that will pass away. A fresh perspective will give us the jolt of endurance to go about our day without worrying over the petty or fleeting. Instead, we will focus on living as examples to those around us

> and encourage them that this world is not the end. Everything we do as ministry and as worship to the Lord in the here and now has eternal value. One day, in God's ultimate timing, He will bring about a new heaven and a new Earth to bring about the full reality of His kingdom for eternity. (See Revelation 21.) Until then, as we allow God to work in and through us, we have kingdom impact. Let this future reality soothe our troubled hearts during our present trials and troubles.

We all have a choice to make in how we spend our emotional and physical energy each day. If we spend it on heavenly pursuits, our King is lifted high in our lives. If we spend it on earthly pursuits, we will find ourselves running in circles. Living out our commitment to the kingship of Christ ensures that our perspectives are set and our hearts and minds are focused on worshipping and obeying the One who makes our world go round.

I invite you to join in with the author of our psalm as he expresses his awe and wonder of his—and our—eternal God.

> *All creation will stand in awe of You,* O Eternal One.
> Thanks will pour from *the mouths of* every one of Your creatures;
> Your holy people will bless You.
> *They will not be silent;* they will talk of the grandeur of Your kingdom
> and celebrate *the wonder of* Your power . . .
> Your kingdom will never end;
> Your rule will endure forever. (Ps. 145:10–11, 13)

My friend Nicole and I took some time to encourage each other in developing our kingdom perspectives. Her thoughts will help us begin to wrap our minds around the concept.

SARAH What are your thoughts about "living Kingdom minded," where we live with things eternal rather than things of this earth as our main priority?

NICOLE I think living kingdom minded is so incredibly important. When we are focused on eternity, and I mean focused—zeroing-in-on, tunnel vision type focused—our perspectives are altered in a powerful way. Not only are we able to see the urgency and intensity of what is at stake for those around us who don't know the Lord, but we also live our lives in a different way.

I can't agree more. That is why I'm so captivated by the idea of "doing life differently." Keeping kingdom focus enables us to figure out just how to do that everyday. It is all too tempting to allow the "here and now" of life, the drama, the relationship woes, the heartache to block our view from the eternal perspective that everything works for our good when we follow Jesus with our hearts, minds, souls, and strength (see Romans 8:28; Luke 10:27). But if we will submit to Him on the road toward the eternal, our present reality of God's kingdom will keep us in a mind frame where we embrace God's grace, joy, truth, forgiveness, and mercy as He transforms us to look more and more like Jesus.

Nicole reinforced this thought process during our conversation when she said, "When we have an eternal perspective, the smaller things in life that would normally stress us out can be handled gracefully because we see that every situation and circumstance we encounter on this earth is a means to an end, a glorious end." No matter what age you are or what stage of life, we all have room for transformation. We start anew every New Year. We also start anew when life circumstances change. I think as we decide to RISE UP!, we have a cool opportunity to start anew spiritually and begin our transformation.

I hope you will take these words from Nicole to heart just as I have: "I honestly believe that the only way to live with an eternal, kingdom perspective is to be in the presence of Jesus constantly. To walk with Him, talk with Him, spend time with Him, love Him, be loved by Him, just breathe Him in. This type of perspective won't just happen because we want it to. It takes steady discipline of bringing ourselves into His presence." That's so true. The temptation is to jump into our day without rechecking our perspective, when what we really need is to get into God's presence so he can realign our thinking. If I'm left up to my own devices, I live my day with a Sarah-focused perspective. Things like envy, inadequacy, and grasping for "things" instead of clinging to my King all deter my focus, turning it inward instead of encouraging an outward focus on thankfulness and on kingdom pursuits.

Have meaningful conversations with Jesus. This is where the rubber meets the road.

In this chapter we will further unpack the kingdom perspective. I know you will be encouraged to know that we live in a kingdom that will never be shaken. You will see that a kingdom perspective helps us focus on what is truly important in life. We will also explore the role of prayer. We've much work to do together in this chapter. Hang tight. Make time for the journal prompts. Have meaningful conversations with Jesus. This is where the rubber meets the road.

- ☐ Write out your own definition of a kingdom perspective.
- ☐ What challenges do you face (or might you anticipate) in living with a kingdom perspective? (Example: People might not "get" you or think you are weird.)
- ☐ List some ways your life presently reveals that you have even a bit of kingdom perspective.
- ☐ Are you ready for a time of spiritual transformation to help you become more like Jesus? How do you see this going hand in hand with a kingdom perspective?

RISE UP! in Prayer

In the pages of your journal, finish this prayer prompt with your own words.

- Father God, I choose to place my focus on Your kingdom today in these ways . . .
- Help me to change my perspective . . .
- You are worthy of my worship. I pray that you would transform me to be more like You today.

Thy Kingdom Come

Every night at summer camp, our counselor would lead us in the Lord's Prayer as we drifted off to sleep. With the balmy night surrounding us as we lay on our beds in screened-in cabins, the sweet sound of young girls' voices echoed along the lakeside of that camp in Texas. I remember hearing the crickets sing and the waves gently hitting the lakeshore as all stood right in my nine-year-old world.

We would recite the prayer in the traditional, Elizabethan English . . .

> Our Father, who art in heaven
> hallowed be Thy Name;
> Thy kingdom come, Thy will be done
> on earth as it is in heaven.
> Give us this day our daily bread,
> and forgive us our trespasses
> as we forgive those who trespass against us;
> and lead us not into temptation,
> but deliver us from evil.
> For Thine is the kingdom, the power, and the
> glory for ever and ever. Amen.

What is interesting is that my summer camp wasn't a "Christian camp." We didn't listen to Bible stories in between canoeing lessons or swim time. The Lord's Prayer was a good, generic prayer in which everyone could partake. One day, for me, that "generic" prayer would mean more than just memories of summer camp, praying in Elizabethan English as we drifted off to sleep after a long day of fun in the sun. One day, the Lord's Prayer would teach me that God's kingdom will come and that I have a role to play in it.

Let's take some time to look at what the phrase "thy kingdom come" means. The Lord's Prayer comes from Matthew 6, where Jesus takes time to teach His disciples to pray. We will cover prayer more extensively in the next chapter, but I couldn't help but bring in the Lord's Prayer as we talk about living with a kingdom perspective. Imagine yourself sitting with Jesus as one of His disciples and learning how to talk to God. Imagine learning this from God Himself! Jesus lived in constant conversation with the Father, and this constant conversation is something we, too, can participate in. This is part of what living with a kingdom perspective means—understanding that we simply must communicate with our Lord in order to live out our faith.

Jesus prayed in Matthew 6:9–10:

> Our Father in heaven,
> let Your name remain holy.
> Bring about Your kingdom.
> Manifest Your will here on earth,
> as it is manifest in heaven.

With a kingdom perspective, we live lives of praise by keeping the name of God holy in our hearts and in our speech. He is holy anyway, regardless of whether or not we elevate Him in our lives. But, we have the opportunity to take part in the grand plans of the kingdom when we allow that holy perspective to seep into every part of our day-to-day existence. We, too, become holy when we declare Jesus as our Lord and Savior. He made us holy and acceptable in God's presence with the blood shed on the cross.

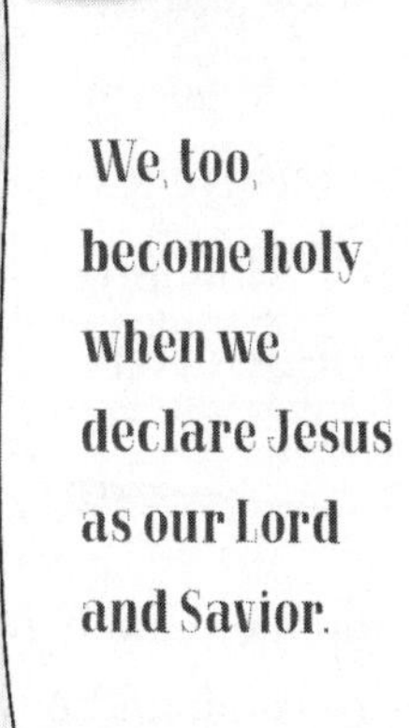
We, too, become holy when we declare Jesus as our Lord and Savior.

- What ways do we step away from that holiness as we go about our day?
- Are we thinking about His holiness when we are tempted to willingly sin?

- Are we thinking about His holiness when we make choices leading us toward His kingdom work? Or are we leaning toward our own agendas?
- Are we thinking about His holiness throughout our day as we make time to connect with Him in worship and prayer? Or do we check that box in the morning during quiet time and then neglect to revisit worship in our day?

Just as Jesus prayed that God's name remain holy, may we allow His name to remain our focus as we RISE UP! each day with kingdom perspective.

In the next verse of Jesus' prayer, He asked that God's kingdom would come. One day we will see the beauty of heaven, but in the meantime we can welcome the kingdom of God here on earth. That present reality of the kingdom of God boosts my morale on the days when life gets tough. When circumstances seem too much to bear, I think come soon, Lord Jesus! There will be a day when Jesus returns in person. That day will be unlike anything we can imagine. As you grow closer and closer to Jesus, that yearning for Him to come soon will boost your kingdom perspective. As you look around the world and see the need for His holiness, you will begin a practice of rejoicing in the fact that you can experience His goodness right now as you yearn for that future kingdom.

Hearts are hurting and desperate for the hope and forgiveness that only Jesus offers.

This is where an interesting paradox occurs. Yes, a few sentences ago I said that we can welcome the kingdom of God here on earth. There is beauty of which to partake in heaven to come and on this earth here and now. But, there is also a great need here and now for people to know Jesus. Hearts are hurting and desperate for the hope and forgiveness that only Jesus offers. On one hand we hope and pray for God's kingdom to come soon, for Jesus to return. On the other hand, we have a part in that kingdom manifesting here on earth, right at this moment.

If we desire to RISE UP!, we must each live a life that proclaims Jesus as King of kings. We must walk in obedience to His word. We must go about our day so that people can't help but notice that Jesus is living in us. His love, His Word, His praise, His goodness, His mercy, His hope just spill out of us. Our part in the unfolding of God's kingdom here on earth is that we live with a kingdom perspective and proclaim His fame.

We won't always do this perfectly. No, there will be times when we drop the ball or we choose our own fame or desires over God's kingdom. From time to time, we will royally mess up. There is great opportunity in those mess-ups, though. It is when we admit to our sins and ask forgiveness of those we hurt that we are examples of Christ's forgiveness to those who've yet to call Him Savior. When we readily own up to the fact that we are not perfect, others see our need for Jesus and hopefully realize their own need. Living with kingdom perspective doesn't mean we walk in our own perfection, but rather, we live in the perfect holiness of Jesus, who makes us holy. We may then extend that perfect forgiveness towards others. May we RISE UP! and admit our imperfection. May we RISE UP! and make the perfection of Jesus known.

Take some time with the journal prompts below to solidify what "thy kingdom come" means to you.

Journal 2
THY KINGDOM COME

In your Bible, flip to Hebrews 10:10. I want us to focus on the idea that we are made perfect and holy only because of Jesus and the cross. Write out this verse in your journal. This will help you really engage with Scripture.

Your translation may use the word "sanctified" instead of "holy." Being sanctified or holy means that we are "set apart." We are called to live differently after we accept Jesus in our hearts as savior. This holiness is a gift, and with it, we can partake in God's kingdom work!

- ☐ What are your thoughts on Hebrews 10:10 and the idea that we are made holy through Jesus? How does this affect your thoughts about rising up and making Jesus famous? Does it take some of the pressure off because you don't have to do this in your own strength?
- ☐ We talked about the concept of "thy kingdom come." Do you ever have a yearning for heaven? To see Jesus face-to-face? If you don't have this yearning, it is okay! This is a heart condition that will develop as you grow in your relationship with God. What are your thoughts on the phrase "thy kingdom come on earth"?

RISE UP! in Prayer

Take some time to finish this prayer prompt with your own words in the space below.

- Father God, give me a heart that yearns for Your kingdom . . .
- Forgive me, Lord, for times that I step away from kingdom perspective and live for my own agenda . . .
- Help me look for ways in my life to further Your kingdom . . .

A Kingdom Never Shaken

Have you ever had a tough conversation with . . . yourself? Once during a workout session with my friend Harmony, we were soaked in sweat and lifting heavy dumbbells when Harmony made a joke about my all-out need for a regimen—a clear-cut schedule—in order to thrive. Harmony, ever the free spirit and one who embraces life right in the moment, made a lighthearted joke. But her words of truth meandered back into my thoughts after the workout, and it made me angry. But I was not angry at her. I was angry at myself for my rigid nature. If you are one who doesn't necessarily need a firm schedule to navigate your day, my hat is off to you. I personally need a black-and-white routine to follow, and as I reflected on this conversation, I realized I need the routine so as not to fly off course. I am most productive when each puzzle piece of my day fits tightly into place. Mess up that puzzle, and I become a disorganized mess!

When we stand on the firm foundation of God's kingdom, we can outright let go of our need to handle life.

I think what aroused such anger was that I do, in fact, have this deep-down desire to be flexible, to be free, to not live tied to anything, but to enjoy each moment here and now. I want to just breathe in fresh air and go where the wind blows me that day. I have a yearning to release the knot of rigidity. I truly do want to be willing and ready, hands thrown up in surrender, to go where God wants me to go—regardless of what's on my schedule. The problem is that I don't always know how to release that knot of rigidity. Now that I've uncovered this never-before-noticed desire within me, I will start to take those breaths of fresh air and stand today with my hands unclenched. When we stand on the firm foundation of God's kingdom, we can outright let go of our need to handle life.

Whether you are the rigid-schedule type like me or the free spirit like my friend Harmony, I think we can all benefit from the truth expressed in

Hebrews 12:28–29. We all need the assurance that we are called to stand firm in God's unshakable kingdom as we take our place and follow where God leads us. Maybe a balance is sometimes needed. Maybe there is a time and a place to breathe in fresh air and live free in order to experience God's goodness right in the moment. On the flip side, maybe there are times when our reliable (sometimes rigid) nature reminds others of God's unshakable, never-changing character and kingdom. They know they can count on us in times of need. All facets of our character traits shine light on God's kingdom when we live in this truth . . .

> Therefore, let us all be thankful that we are a part of an unshakable Kingdom and offer to God worship that pleases Him and reflects the awe and reverence we have toward Him, for He is like a fierce fire that consumes everything. (Heb. 12:28–29)

Be encouraged that God's presence, His kingdom, will not be touched or ruined or shaken by anything of this world. For everything of the world is under God's command. This means for us that when we stand firm on the heavenly, solid kingdom, when we trust that God's ways are better, He is in control even if life around us seems like a wild carnival ride. We don't have to live on a perpetual roller coaster—allowing life to twist our faith. We have God's kingdom to keep us grounded. Uncertainties of life make some days feel like that roller coaster, with ups and downs and our hair flying wildly in the wind. People will let us down. We will have questions about why bad things happen. Yet, we are not meant to be influenced and swept up by the uncertainties but, rather, to approach each day with the gratitude that Hebrews 12:28 calls for. As we take note of the twists and turns and the ups and downs in the moment, we need to remember that God has gifted us with His never-shaken kingdom as our home base—our place to stand that never changes. When we make the choice to stand firm in God's kingdom with awe and reverence of His sovereignty and power, God is blessed, for we have chosen to worship Him. The act of standing firm in Him is pure praise of the name of Jesus when our compass points due North toward the kingdom perspective. At each twist and turn of the roller coaster of uncertainty, we have a decision to make: live wobbly in this uncertain life or stand firm in the unshakable Kingdom.

— **In this uncertain life** . . . your world seems to crumble when your parents' marriage fizzles into divorce. Your whole life, including every person you've counted on since birth, seems amiss in this new normal. You may be tempted to isolate yourself from your family.

— But in the firm foundation of the kingdom . . . Jesus is the glue that holds your life together. He will never leave you nor forsake you (Heb. 13:5). You can stand firm and continue to love and serve your family regardless of the new dynamic.

— **In this uncertain life** . . . your precious child is in the hospital with symptoms that doctors can't yet diagnose and IVs and medicine and needles are in abundance. You feel as if your hands are tied. Sleep deprived and filled with fear, you just can't understand why God would allow your little one such pain.

— But in the firm foundation of the kingdom . . . you need never doubt that your mighty God knows, sees, cares, loves, and heals. He is holding your sweet one in His hands (Isa. 41:10).

— **In this uncertain life** . . . the economy tumbles and your company announces layoffs. You are the new person in the office, so chances are you will be without a job very soon. Fear, uncertainty, and thoughts of desperate finances set in.

— But in the firm foundation of the kingdom . . . you can be confident that God will fill every need you have; He knows what you need before you even ask Him (Phil. 4:19; Matt. 6:8).

— **In this uncertain life** . . . the values we held tight to as a kid come into question as cultural issues, like gay marriage, abortion, and legalized marijuana (just to name a few), arise. What used to be right-side up regarding what we believe may now seem topsy-turvy.

— But in the firm foundation of the Kingdom . . . God's Word remains unshakable and will never mislead us. God's ways are higher than our ways, even when we just don't understand why (Isa. 55:9 NKJV).

Make your decision right here and now on where you will choose to stand. Where will you decide to plant your feet? Will you place them in the unpredictable world around you, or on God's firm, unshakable foundation?

While you are making the choice where to stand, I wonder if you would RISE UP! with a kingdom perspective if you experienced for yourself the sensation of standing on a faith, a solid kingdom, that will not be shaken. Would you take a stand for the fame of Jesus if you knew the eternal effects of proclaiming His name? Would you speak of His awesome works in your life if you knew that the hearts around you live desperate for hope and freedom? Would you take on the hard role of leadership in forging the way with your peers if you knew the eternal ramifications of loving and serving others in the name of Jesus?

We can only live out our faith with bold abandonment if we know just what we stand.

All of these heart-piercing questions are meant to lead us to evaluate what we believe. We can only live out our faith with bold abandonment if we know just what we stand. We can make a big impact if we actually declare what we believe with that same boldness. Sometimes our declarations will manifest in actual words, and sometimes they will manifest in the life choices we make, the things we choose or choose not to do.

I decided to sit down and take my own advice and scribble out my bold declarations of the kingdom and on what exactly I stand firm. You should have seen me with my cute pink-and-turquoise composition notebook and pen as I sat in the coffee shop furiously writing for a good ten minutes. This kind of thinking gets my heart pumping with excitement. Take a look at my personal RISE UP! declarations.

- I believe the Bible is God's Holy Word, which is without error, incapable of being wrong and applicable to every part of my life. I will read it, soak in it regularly and actually live it out.
- I believe that Jesus died on the cross to forgive my sins and allow me the path to an intimate relationship with the almighty God for all eternity as well as right here and right now in my life. I also believe that three days later, He rose victorious from the dead and sits on His throne in heaven.
- I believe that we live in a fallen, sin-filled world. I, too, sin daily, yet I do not live in condemnation, but, rather, in the forgiveness of Jesus.
- I believe that the only way to an eternal relationship with God is by a saving faith in Jesus Christ.
- I believe that because I've declared Jesus as my Lord and Savior, His Holy Spirit lives in my heart. It is my desire to live my life always sensitive to God's presence in my life and to follow the leading of the Spirit. This requires daily decisions to put aside my selfishness and choose to partake in God's kingdom.
- I believe that one day (hopefully soon!) Jesus will come back to this earth and all will be right in His world again. I believe, according to God's word, He will establish His eternal kingdom and defeat the devil once and for all. Until then, I will stand on the promise of His coming victory and refuse to allow the devil a foot in my life.

- I believe that until the day of His coming I have an important role in the kingdom to proclaim the fame of Jesus. I will live out my faith with reverence and commitment.
- I believe that my King is ready and willing to pour out His grace and forgiveness when I temporarily step away from my kingdom role and live with my own agenda in mind.
- I believe that by serving others I am serving the King. Everyday I will think of others before myself.

I admit that these belief statements and declarations add up to one tall order. Yes, they are difficult to fulfill on my own strength, but I've come to realize that with a kingdom perspective comes the realization that God is the one who works these declarations out in our lives if we choose to stand firm in Him. He is the one who nudges me daily toward His Word and sets my heart straight when there is an opportunity to love others. He is the one who did the work on the Cross. It is my daily decision to make, though, to allow the Spirit of God to do His thing in my heart and life as I RISE UP!

> **Let's be women who know what we believe and stand firm regardless of what life brings.**

I encourage you to take some time with the following journal prompts to make your own belief statements. Make the choice to not be irresponsible and unsure, but to be a woman who knows what she believes and stands firm regardless of what life brings. You have no idea what impression you will make when others see you standing firm. People around you will take notice of your authenticity and conviction. Take advantage of this and RISE UP! to make Jesus famous.

Journal 3
A KINGDOM NEVER SHAKEN

Take a few minutes and read through this passage in Matthew 7:

> Those people who are listening to Me, those people who *hear what I say and* live according to My teachings—you are like a wise man who built his house on a rock, *on a firm foundation. When storms hit,* rain pounded down and waters rose, *levies broke* and winds beat all the walls of that house. But the house did not fall because it was built upon rock. Those of you who are listening and do not hear—you are like a fool who builds a house on sand. When a storm comes to his house, *what will happen?* The rain will fall, the waters will rise, the wind will blow, and his house will collapse with a great crash.
>
> With that Jesus finished His teaching, and the crowds were amazed by all He had said. But Jesus taught in His own name, on His own authority, not like the scribes. (vv. 24–29)

- [ ] What are some examples of times when the "storm" came through and threatened your belief system or how you feel about God?
- [ ] How do you see value in building your faith and your life on the firm foundation of God's kingdom? If this is a tough one for you, take some time to write out your questions or doubts.

Now for the exciting and challenging part! Let's work on our bold declarations. A prayer before we dive in . . .

Father God, enlighten our minds to the truth on which you want us to stand firm. Give us courage to write out what we believe and then actually live it! Amen!

Use my prompts below to get you started . . .

- ☐ What do I believe about sin and the world I live in? (See Genesis 3.)
- ☐ What do I believe about my personal sin and need for forgiveness? (See Romans 3:21–26.)
- ☐ What do I believe about the cross and the resurrection of Jesus? (See Luke 22–24 or any of the accounts in Matthew, Mark, or John.)
- ☐ What will I declare about my personal acceptance of Jesus as my Lord and Savior?
- ☐ What do I believe about the Bible and the relevance of God's Word in my life? (See Hebrews 4:12.)
- ☐ What do I believe about the importance of serving others in the name of Jesus? (See Matthew 25:31–46.)
- ☐ What do I believe is my role in the kingdom of God? (See Luke 10:27.)

I encourage you to not rush through this exercise and to take time with the suggested scripture. If you get to a place where you can't state what you believe, talk to a pastor or someone strong in his or her faith.

I'm excited for you as you make these bold statements. Be ready to RISE UP! and allow God to move in your life as you live out what you believe.

What Really Matters

If you were to walk into my storage closet, you would see an embarrassingly large stack of old magazines. There are times when I'm seduced by the allure of the perfect figures on the magazine covers promising a fit body, perfectly shiny hair, or a fantastic sex life if I only follow the few quick steps in that particular article. Yes. I am easily swept up in those fitness, fashion and self-help magazines. But if what they promise is supposed to be "end all," then why the need for a magazine article each month restating in a new, fresh way what the articles the month before pronounced? It is an endless cycle.

> **We find ourselves going in endless circles around the things of the world in an attempt to find what only God can provide.**

During the times when I was not immersed in God's Word and seeking His kingdom, I was still seeking Him, yet I didn't know it. I sought fulfillment in shopping—spending money to experience the thrill of something new. I looked to food to satisfy my taste, yet I didn't look to the One who could ultimately satiate the needs of my heart. I looked to the headlines of the self-help magazines to lead me to some sort of answer to a question I really didn't know my heart desperately asked . . .

WHAT MATTERS MOST?

Those who make money and print the magazines know that every human is looking for answers to the question of what matters most. They proclaim the answers in the form of various marketing campaigns and perfectly placed products to entice us in our emptiness. We find ourselves going in endless circles around the things of the world in an attempt to find what only God can provide. Only when I am soaking in the truth and the answers God provides in His Word, can I stop running, stop striving, stop spending, stop overeating, and sit in the peace that Jesus provides. When I sit quietly with His kingdom in mind, I find the answer to my questions.

I am a fairly black-and-white kind of person, and I love it when things are spelled out for me. I especially love it when God provides a checklist of sorts in scripture, as in Matthew 22:37–39, where Jesus was asked what is the greatest commandment.

> Jesus said to him, "'You shall love the LORD your God with all your heart, with all your soul, and with all your mind.' This is the first and great commandment. And the second is like it: 'You shall love your neighbor as yourself.'" (NKJV)

What especially attracts me to Jesus' answer is that everything in life can be put into two buckets:

1. Loving God with all my heart, soul and mind
2. Loving my neighbor as myself

I can focus on what matters most in my career if I measure it by whether I'm loving God by working for Him with integrity and with all my might. I can focus on what matters most in my finances if I live to please God and find fulfillment in Him rather than in retail therapy. I can also focus on what matters most if I'm treating my body with respect because I love the One who created me.

Second, I can fit my relationships and the way I interact with others in the bucket of loving others as myself—the second part of Jesus' commandment. When in an argument with my loved one, I should ask the question, does what we are arguing about really matter long term? Also, when I'm convicted that my world is revolving around my personal needs in a manner that puts me off-kilter with Jesus, I turn to doing something, anything, to serve someone else—to put that person's needs above my own.

If we truly desire to make Jesus famous, then it is imperative that we live out the greatest commandment. We can only RISE UP! effectively if we evaluate our heart condition daily. Where does my mind wander? Is my soul satisfied in God's kingdom alone? Oh, it is easy to get off track, especially when we find ourselves in a weak moment, maybe on a day when He is not on the forefront of our minds. Jesus offers us a fresh start the moment we confess that we've looked to our own selfish desires over His kingdom. I believe a characteristic of a woman with mature faith is the ability to quickly see when she has gotten off track and hurry back to the throne of her King.

In our quest to focus more on what matters most, we can take our cue from the author of Psalm 145, David, and his attitude toward God's kingdom. Throughout this psalm, David expressed his understanding of an ultimate truth: God's kingdom endures forever, no matter what fleeting life circumstances or human mishaps occur across the expanse of time.

Jesus offers us a fresh start the moment we confess that we've looked to our own selfish desires over His kingdom.

> Your kingdom is an everlasting kingdom,
> And Your dominion endures throughout all
> generations.
> (Ps. 145:13 NKJV)

- When atrocious events shake our world, God's power and kingdom are still everlasting.
- When those we love break our hearts into a million pieces, God's love and kingdom are still everlasting.
- When we don't agree with decisions that our politicians make on our behalf, God's knowledge and kingdom are still everlasting.
- When our bank accounts are empty, God's provision and kingdom are still everlasting.

Only a kingdom perspective, knowing that we are part of the bigger picture, can answer the question of what matters most. We take part in something bigger than ourselves when we recognize the need to love Jesus and serve others with every fiber of our beings. This takes an increased measure of trust as we step out of our comfort zone and make bold choices in our lives. What would happen if we stepped far out on a limb and looked beyond our selfish desires in life and instead chose actions that have an eternal impact? We have this opportunity daily, should we choose to resolve that God's kingdom is everlastingly our priority. Let us rearrange our thoughts and our heart condition to seek how we fit into this bigger picture and focus less on that which doesn't meet our needs. I guarantee you will find the answers to your questions of life's purpose, self-identity, and what matters most.

Take some time using the journal prompts to converse with the Lord about how you can live out this ultimate truth of what matters most: the kingdom of God.

Journal 4
WHAT REALLY MATTERS

Let's dig deep into our hearts and evaluate how we live out the greatest commandment.

- ☐ In your journal, write out Matthew 27:37–39 verbatim from your Bible.
- ☐ What does it mean for you to love God with all your heart and soul? What things in your life might you put above Jesus or might you turn to instead of Him?
- ☐ How can you rearrange your thoughts in order to love God with all your mind? (Feel free to flip back to chapter 1 where we talked about living a life of praise. Many thoughts can be transformed by choosing to simply praise Jesus.)

Join me in evaluating a few areas of life where we might easily get off track and focus more on ourselves rather than God's kingdom. In each of the other areas that follow, think about one way you can love God with all your heart, soul, and mind AND serve others. I will give an example to get you started.

- ☐ Career: (Example: How can you work with more integrity at your job? How do the words you use at work reflect your love for Jesus? Would people be surprised to know you attend church?)
- ☐ Raising children: (Example: What are some times when you should put the needs of your family above your own personal needs? What is an example of a place where you can truly live out what you believe as an example to your children?)
- ☐ Money: (Example: Do you go on shopping sprees and spend your money when you feel dissatisfied with life? When you're low on

money, what is your level of trust that God will provide? How can you be more generous with your money, even when things might seem tight? Or when there is an abundance, are you willing to give?)

- ☐ Body image: (Example: Do you take good care of your body because it is God's beautiful creation?)
- ☐ Friendships and family relationships: (Example: Do you honor your friends by stepping away from gossip? Do you respect your parents even as an adult?)
- ☐ Romantic relationships: (Example: If you are married, do you serve and respect your husband? If you are single or dating, do you keep Jesus as your priority even though the lovey-dovey feelings of romance are so enticing?)
- ☐ Other: What's another area of your life where you can love God with your entire being and serve others?
- ☐ What is one way you can get out and serve someone else? Take a look at the mission ministries at your church and within your community.

RISE UP! in Prayer

Take some time to finish this prayer prompt with your own words.

- Father God, I ask today for a heart to seek out what matters most . . . your kingdom . . .
- Lord, when I get off track in these areas, bring me back to a kingdom perspective . . .

Do Life Differently

The word urgent comes to mind when I think of our quest to RISE UP! For me, I thrive on the adrenaline that comes with urgency. It is when I work best. A deadline approaching gets my blood flowing, and the excitement and expectancy of what is urgent in life boosts my energy. The problem with adrenaline rushes is that they are short-lived. It is easy to get all geared up for a crisis and then allow my attention to wane when the sense of urgency dies down.

There is a call for our generation to get off the couch of complacency and do life differently with a kingdom perspective in the forefront of our thinking and motivation. The kingdom of God in it's ultimate fulfillment is fast approaching. Jesus is coming! There is work to do in the meantime, and we will miss out on experiencing the glory of God for ourselves if we sit back and just live out the status quo. Let us take our place in the movement of God with a sense of urgency. We must be keyed into what God is doing among this world of chaos. We must be engaged in the work of the kingdom and not get caught up in activities or ways of thinking that are not kingdom productive.

There is a call for our generation to get off the couch of complacency and do life differently with a kingdom perspective.

We can talk about big-picture ideas of the kingdom, but I think it first starts with our decision to make different kinds of choices in the nuts and bolts of our daily life. What are little decisions we make everyday that are in continuity with a kingdom perspective? Are there any activities that we partake in that cause us to stumble back into our self-focus? When we choose to RISE UP! with abandonment for the kingdom, living differently from the ways of the world is not a casual request from God. No, it is a command straight from the pages of Scripture.

> *So it comes down to this:* since you have been raised with the Anointed One, *the Liberating King,* set your mind on heaven above. The Anointed is there, seated at God's right hand. Stay focused on what's above, not on earthly things, because your *old* life is dead and gone. Your *new* life is now hidden, enmeshed with the Anointed who is in God. On that day when the Anointed One—who is our very life—is revealed, you will be revealed with Him in glory! (Col. 3:1–4)

Doing life differently means we recognize our role in this kingdom. Just as Paul explained in the passage above, we must stay focused on what has eternal purpose rather than the fleeting and shallow pleasures of this world. This does not mean we shy away from fun. It does mean, however, that we constantly evaluate the way we do life. Do our daily activities steer us toward an everlasting focus or toward that which fades away and steals our joy?

I'd like for us to return to my conversation with my friend Nicole. I asked Nicole to give us some examples of bold life choices she makes in order to do life differently with a kingdom perspective. I call these bold life choices even though they might seem like little tweaks we make in life. It is those little life tweaks that can be the hardest to adjust.

Please know, the concept of how to live with heavenly focus is different for each of us. The choices I tweak in my life are things that I personally need to change in order to steer my focus back to Christ. Those stumbling blocks of mine may not be your stumbling blocks. Keep this in mind as we consider some of the ways we may adjust our lives to keep a kingdom perspective.

In a moment we will take some time to look at a verse of scripture that encourages us to keep our focus on heavenly pursuits instead of things of this earth. Our actions and life choices reflect our belief system. We must choose to invest time and energy in the kingdom. In the bold act of making tough life choices—to cut out or add certain activities or thought processes to our life—we glorify the name of Jesus. Because we know this

Earth is fleeting, we invest in the eternal with the sheer motivation that this pleases our King Jesus and furthers His kingdom.

Doing life differently is not an easy task. Some people might think we are weird because of the choices we make. We may have to sacrifice partaking in activities that we once thought brought us pleasure because we realize that they put us in a compromising position. But I envision women across the world taking a stand with firm faith, going against the grain, rising up and turning heads as people ask why she . . .

- chooses NOT to live with her boyfriend and have sex before marriage
- chooses NOT to allow images in the media to distract her attention from appreciating her husband
- chooses NOT to use "OMG" language (see chapter 1)
- chooses NOT to participate in gossip with friends or at the office
- chooses TO love, respect, and submit to her husband or her future husband and to pray for him regularly
- chooses TO go out and vote during election season and take a stand for biblical values
- chooses TO be generous with her money, giving out of love for Jesus, even when it is a sacrifice
- chooses TO invest her time in serving others even if it is a sacrifice
- chooses TO tell a friend she will pray for him or her and then actually pray right there on the spot
- chooses TO seek God's direction for life changes and then be brave in faith and take the next steps

Will you be a part of this movement of women who RISE UP! and live differently? Will you make some tough life changes? Be bold. Be brave in faith. Be confident that you serve a mighty God who is worth the sacrifices you might make.

DO LIFE DIFFERENTLY

- ☐ In your own Bible, read Colossians 3:1–4 and 2 Corinthians 4:16–18.
- ☐ Brainstorm ways that you can make little, yet bold life tweaks in order to live with a kingdom perspective.
- ☐ After reading this chapter and working through the Bible study journal prompts for each section, do you see value in the "eternal things" versus the "earthly things"? What are ways you can live out these passages from Colossians and 2 Corinthians?
- ☐ Pray this prayer with me:

Father God, we desire Your kingdom and Your fame to be known throughout our world. Touch our hearts in a special way to show us how we can do life differently and live out our faith. Give us courage when these life tweaks seem hard or weird by the world's standards. May we see the benefit of Your kingdom over the fading, shallow pleasures of this world. In Jesus' name, amen!

Notes

Notes

CHAPTER THREE

Bow low Before you RISE UP!

Now that we are in the thick of our topic of rising up to make Jesus famous in our lives, it is time to get to some really tough material. In this chapter we will challenge each other to take on a posture of humility by physically, emotionally, and spiritually bowing low before our King Jesus. Our Lord did it first as He lived as our example of a servant. Though He could have deservedly lived a life of power and authority, instead Jesus came to serve (Matt. 20:28; Phil. 2).

In this chapter we will find encouragement in Scripture to bow low before Jesus so we can RISE UP! and bring Him glory. The key is that we set our hearts in the right place.

John the Baptist said it beautifully: "He must increase, but I must decrease" (John 3:30 NKJV).

> He must increase in my heart as my King and ultimate authority.
> I must decrease and relent my stubborn ways of running my own life.
> He must increase in my mind as I praise Him in every situation.
> I must decrease in my spoiled complaining and whining throughout my day.

He must increase in my life as I look to please Him alone in everything I do.

I must decrease as I evaluate the ways I spend my time and look for happiness.

In order to RISE UP!, I encourage you to decrease.

It will be uncomfortable. But let's get on our knees. Let's get on our faces before the Lord. And let's set our hearts in a place that makes us ready to allow Him to work through us as we RISE UP!

"He must increase, but I must decrease." (John 3:30 NKJV)

Humility goes against the grain of society as we daily participate in acts like celebrity worship. It also goes against our own personal, human tendencies. We are usually taught to look out for ourselves and to elevate and puff up our image. Ironically, it takes a ton of work and effort to keep up with this cultural and personal agenda of making our own names famous. It is hard work to keep up appearances on Facebook and take beautiful pictures of our "perfect" life on Instagram. Making sure that we always look like we have it all together is a job in itself if we allow it to be our life's driving force. Though serving others—putting their needs above our own—is tough work, too, it relieves us of the pressure of performance. Yes, bowing low before Jesus in submission to His ultimate authority puts us in a posture of vulnerability. (We will talk more about that in this chapter.) Scripture clearly states that the King of the universe, the God almighty, raises up those who bow before Him in every part of their life. Let us bow before our King Jesus, presenting Him with humble hearts ready to be led by His perfect hand. He is worthy of our reverence.

Now join me in a Facebook conversation I held with some friends who do life and Bible study together in Pennsylvania. I appreciate the honesty in this conversation, and I hope you, too, will put aside any preconceived notions of the concept of bowing low before God as we RISE UP!.

SARAH Hey friends, get ready for a pretty heady topic. Hope you don't mind me picking your brain. I would love to know what first comes to mind when you hear these words bowing low before God.

CYNTHIA I totally love the concept. I've come to view bowing low and actually kneeling before God as figure of speech as well as an actual physical posture. I came from a faith background where we would always pray on our knees. At first I never understood it. Then someone from my church explained it to me. Praying on our knees is a form of sacrifice and respect to my Lord. He has sacrificed enough on our behalf. I also think that taking a physical posture of kneeling leads to an intimate relationship with God.

SARAH Cynthia, I loved that you said that kneeling puts us in a stance of humility and intimacy with God. I agree. By literally taking a posture of kneeling, we are putting our heart in the right place—ready to receive whatever God has for us—not just our own grand plans.

KRISTINE I'd love to chime in on this. Praying on your knees is so uncomfortable—what a parallel to humility. I've realized how strained my relationship with God is. I want Christ to be everything, but I feel like I'm in this fog that I can't see through.

ALISON Kristine, He will meet you right where you are. This type of relationship doesn't come easy. It takes time and commitment. It's not easy for me either. The more we get on our knees, the easier it gets over time.

SARAH Kristine, I hear you when you say that you are struggling right now. When you just show up to the relationship with God, when you just simply make yourself available, He will show up too. He will make Himself known. Keep showing up—especially on your knees in humility, ready to receive His guidance and wisdom. The fog will lift.

Kristine brought up a great point regarding this posture as uncomfortable and a parallel to humility. Yes, being humble can be uncomfortable, as we might have feelings of vulnerability when we relent to God's goodness rather than our own plan for our lives. It is when we get out of our comfort zone that God uses and stretches us.

As our conversation unfolded, Kristine went on to remind us that, "as humans, yes we were created to be in perfect union with God, but sin changed all of that." Just as Eve attempted to follow her own agenda in the garden, and take control, we do the same! How often do we put ourselves first, our desires and our comfort as top priority? I'm personally challenged today by the thought of rearranging my priorities and taking a kneeling posture before the Lord It takes discipline on our part to recognize God's authority over our life. Over time, He shows us that His authority and power is for our own good. When we walk down the road several paces and then look back at the choices we made with a humble heart, this retrospective view shows us the benefits of placing God over our own desires and agenda. I surely do not downplay the growth and stretching that happens along the way. The act of unclenching pride and control in favor of kneeling before God takes work . . . hard work.

The act of unclenching pride and control in favor of kneeling before God takes work... hard work.

My friend Gwen joined in on the conversation and brought home the concept. She reminded us that "as we grow and mature, we realize just how human we are and how often we fail God, ourselves, and others around us. At the same time, though, we can tell there's definitely a difference in ourselves while we are growing and maturing. And, along with the humility comes a twinge of fear or discomfort because we've been equipped, and now God is stretching us to practice what He has been teaching us."

As you join us in our conversation, take some time with the journal section that follows. Grab your pen and your journal and be open to having personal conversations with Jesus about humility. Allow Him to show you why He is ever so worthy of our posture of bowing low.

Journal 1
BOW LOW BEFORE YOU RISE UP!

Let's check back in with Psalm 145. It may seem repetitious, but trust me. We want to embed scripture in the depths of our minds and allow our hearts to envelop the truth. This is the only way to approach each day, with all of the drama that life throws our way, and effectively RISE UP!

- ☐ As you reread Psalm 145, what verse sticks out to you most? How will you live out this verse and apply it to your life?
- ☐ The words humble and humility will pop up quite often in the rest of this chapter. Dare I say, we will probably have to go to uncomfortable places in our hearts and minds as we allow the Holy Spirit to work on us.
- ☐ What comes to your mind when you read the words humble and humility? Are your thoughts negative or positive?

If you are like me, you probably find that this concept of "bowing low" is tough to live out. It helps to remember that we are not alone. We have One who lived out a perfect example of humility for us to follow.

> *This is the Kingdom's logic:* whoever wants to become great must first make himself a servant; whoever wants to be first must bind himself as a slave—just as the Son of Man did not come to be served, but to serve and to give His life as the ransom for many. (Matt. 20:26–28)

In God's economy, those who are great and first are those who serve others and put aside their own agenda and needs. Jesus came and washed His disciples' feet (John 13:1–17), served living water to a thirsty Samaritan woman (John 4:4–26), and gave Himself as the ultimate sacrifice on the cross.

It is my hope that you will refer back to this journal section throughout this week as you read and chew on the idea of humility and the physical and spiritual concept of bowing low before God. Following are a handful of life scenarios in which you might find yourself with the opportunity to be a humble servant. Use these as a starting place to evaluate throughout the week how you would rearrange your heart, your priorities, and your physical posture to bow low before Jesus as He raises you up. Write out each of the these topics in your journal and leave a few lines of space to fill in later. We will circle back to this list later in the chapter.

These are life areas in which we may need to allow God to work through us. Take an honest look and write out ways you can take a posture of humility.

- ☐ Money: (Example: giving more to your church by tithing, giving even when it hurts your budget because you know God will provide—it is His money. See Proverbs 3:9.)
- ☐ Work Life: (Example: Though there is a time and place to build your résumé and make sure your boss knows you are working hard, how can you change your attitude so that your focus is on doing your work well because it pleases God first? Another example: If you work inside the home, how does the posture of bowing low apply as you serve your family? See Galatians 1:10.)
- ☐ Marriage: (Example: What are ways you can selflessly serve your spouse? If you are not married, how can you mature in your faith with a humble heart in preparation for marriage?)
- ☐ Family Relationships: (Example: It may be difficult to respect your parents if you are struggling to work through hurts from your past. Or, now that you are an adult with your own opinions and worldviews, how can you honor and respect your family?)

- ☐ Friendships: (Example: Learning to be a true friend. This means we love and serve our friends first without expecting them to repay the favor. Is there someone in your group of friends who needs encouragement?)
- ☐ Time: (Example: How can you use your time to serve others in your church or community? Serving others is sacrifice of our time . . . especially our free time.)
- ☐ Day-to-day agenda: (Example: How do you set your goals for each day? Do you take time to sit in prayer and Bible study to humbly seek out God's agenda, or do you power through your day with your own grand plans in mind?)
- ☐ Other: (What are some other areas in your life where you need to allow God to show you how to humble yourself as He raises you up?)

RISE UP! in Prayer

Take some time to finish this prayer prompt with your own words.

- Father God, even if it is difficult for me, show me how I can bow low before your throne in every part of my life . . .
- Dig up areas in my life and convict my soul to take a posture of humility before you . . .

Daniel's Friends and the Fire

THE ONE GOD AND OUR "little g" gods

Though the physical stance of kneeling or posturing facedown before Jesus strikes the world as weird, the concept of bowing down before something—anything—really isn't alien. In fact, we do this everyday to our televisions, when we center our lives around must-see shows, as I very often do. There are many "gods" in our lives to which we inadvertently pay homage, often to the detriment of our relationship with the one God, Jesus. For example, when we put people on a pedestal and worship their seeming perfection, we are in fact bowing low to those people instead of to our King, Jesus. When we focus our thoughts on money and cling so tightly to it that the idea of giving it away makes us sick to our stomachs, we are making money into a "god."

> **Definition of "little g" god: Any thing or any person we elevate above Jesus.**

Bowing low to "little g" gods and giving over our joy, our hope, and our priorities to materials and people robs us of the true fulfillment we gain when we worship God alone. When we bow down to God—and only God—we are not taking a stance that is degrading. The almighty Creator of the universe, who is higher in stature and priority than any "little g" god we might entertain at the moment, sent His son, Jesus, to humbly serve us and then die on the cross for us. God did all of this for you and me so we could stand—could RISE UP!—in His glorious presence.

Join me in the book of Daniel, where we find an exhilarating example of how God raises up those who choose to bow low before God alone. To set the scene, in Daniel 3 we find King Nebuchadnezzar of Babylon, who, caught up in pride and arrogance, commands his servants to build a giant statute made of gold—a "little g" god. This statue was set up on a plain, and all the people of Babylon (The Voice calls them Chaldeans) were commanded to attend the worship of this statue. If anyone defied the king's command, they would immediately face death in a roaring fire. The heroes of our story are Shadrach, Meshach, and Abed-nego—three Israelites and friends of Daniel.

As everyone in the country fell on his or her face before this idol, these brave young men stood in blatant defiance, fully aware of the very dire consequences of their action. They were willing to accept the consequences because they believed their powerful Lord would deliver them from the hot fire, one way or another.

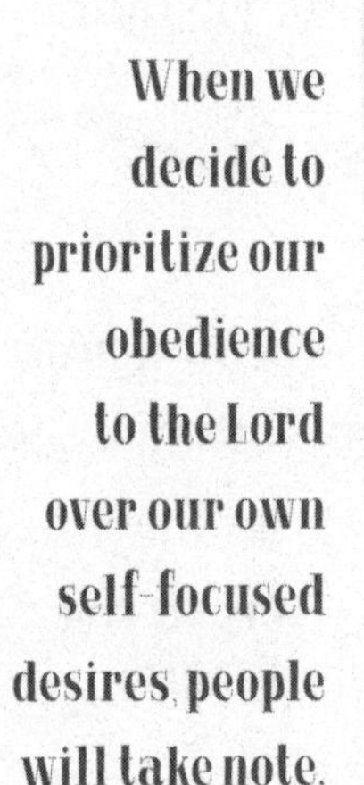
When we decide to prioritize our obedience to the Lord over our own self-focused desires, people will take note.

The large golden image towered over a field of Babylonians. Loud noises of "worship" rang out, cueing every countryman to bow down. The hot fire roared, ready for anyone in defiance. And everyone fell facedown to the ground, probably trying to get even lower for fear they would be seen as not bowing down.

Can you see the three young Israeli men silhouetted as you pan over the field of Babylonians? Can you hear their hearts beating in prayer toward the Lord they faithfully serve, trusting in His protection?

Even though they were ultimately thrown into the fire, not even their hair or clothing was singed. God delivered. King Nebuchadnezzar actually stood astounded and changed his tune, praising the God of Shadrach, Meshach, and Abed-nego. Because they chose to bow low to God alone, because they bravely stood up and did not allow the pressures of the world to deter their laser-focused faith, God used these three young men in a mighty way. A powerful earthly king, who moments before was wrapped up in his own ego, now bowed low before the King of the universe and thus influenced his country to do the same.

At this point, we may not be in danger of a raging fire when we choose to worship God alone, but there are often cultural consequences when we take a humble posture before the Lord. When we decide to prioritize our obedience to the Lord over our own self-focused desires, people will take note. They may not "get" you. The cultural consequences can be subtle and sometimes they are very palpable.

- Your lifestyle of seeking after God rather than chasing ambition pleases God. Those around you may take it as complacency and snub you in the workplace.
- Humility is often taken for weakness. Those who don't love the Lord may attempt to take advantage of your kindness and servant heart.
- Someone with a hurting heart that doesn't know God's love and grace sees Jesus in you. That person may lash out at you out of his or her own pain.
- Family members or old friends who know your past but don't recognize God's redemption in your new story may hold that old baggage against you.
- You might be passed up for a promotion at work because you stand on biblical principles and don't claw your way up the career ladder.

But in God's kingdom the first will be last, and those who serve Him daily, with humble hearts, will experience real, eternal blessings. Take heart; this present consequence of bowing low will pale in comparison to your joy when you bow low before Jesus on His glorious, heavenly throne!

Living an unusual life, making painful life decisions, working through the pressures of the world must not discourage us, for God grants us a holy promise in Scripture. Psalm 145 is like a rally cry for those feeling weary in the journey of making Jesus famous. When our days grow difficult and we face our own fiery furnace, may we find sparks—no, flames—of encouragement as God speaks straight to our need through His everlasting, ever-relevant Word.

> The Eternal sustains all who stumble on their way.

> For those who are broken down, *God is near.* He raises them up *in hope.* (Ps.145:14)

Did you notice our key phrase in this verse? God promises that He will reach His mighty hand down and gently pull us up when we feel that the weight of our life brings us down. All throughout Scripture, God warns us that trials and drama will be a normal part of Christian life. God allows certain events to happen in our lives that we don't understand. He allows us, even when we are serving Him faithfully, to go through pain and struggle. Our faith may begin to waver as our own fiery furnaces seem too much to bear. But just as Daniel's young friends stood tall with firm belief that God was bigger than the fire, we must stand tall with full hope that God raises up those who worship Him alone.

This hope to which we cling means we look past any temporary feelings of discomfort in our present trial and drama, gazing ahead to God's promises of ultimate joy. Let's take that final word, hope, in Psalm 145:14 and pair it with a passage in the book of James.

> Don't run from tests and hardships, brothers and sisters. *As difficult as they are, you will ultimately find joy in them;* if you embrace them, your faith will blossom under pressure *and teach you true patience* as you endure. And true patience brought on by endurance will equip you to complete the long journey *and cross the finish line*—mature, complete, and wanting nothing. (James 1:2–4)

In my personal journey of rising up and living with a kingdom perspective, I've noticed a transformation of my attitude toward painful and difficult circumstances. When I wade past my initial reaction of despair or frustration, when I don't allow myself to go down the road toward self-pity, God shows me that this time of faith testing is worth the present pain or heartache. Over the months and years, that initial snap reaction of despair when unexpected events happen in life has turned into hope and peace and joy, knowing that God is using the present circumstance to build my faith.

This building up of our faith is quite important to God. With His broader, bigger, kingdom perspective, each tough circumstance in our life can be used as a building block. Block by block God builds us up to resist despair or temptations, and readies us to be used by Him in mighty ways for His glory.

This excites me: James encourages us not to run away from the adversities in life. We are to face them head-on. The good news is that we don't have to face life alone. God will never leave us. As we read in Daniel 3, there were not just three men seen in the fiery flames. Four figures walked in that fire.

> Nebuchadnezzar could hardly believe his eyes. Shocked, the king jumped up and asked his advisors,

NEBUCHADNEZZAR Didn't we tie up and throw three men into the heart of the fire?

ADVISORS Yes, O king.

NEBUCHADNEZZAR Then why do I see four men, completely unbound, walking around in the middle of the fire? They don't appear to be hurt at all. And the fourth . . . he appears to be like a son of the gods. (Dan. 3:24–25)

Biblical scholars who have thouroughly interpreted this account say that this fourth figure in the fire was the very presence of God. In fact, it was the fulfillment of the promise God made in Isaiah 43:2. In Isaiah the Lord says:

> When you face *stormy* seas I will be there with you *with endurance and calm;*
> you will not be engulfed in *raging* rivers.

> If *it seems like* you're walking through fire with flames *licking at your limbs,*
> *keep going;* you won't be burned.

God stood strong with those brave young men as they made the choice to worship Him alone. In the same way, we can trust that when we choose to live life with the main goal of honoring Jesus, when we stick our necks out and live differently, God stands right there with us. I can only imagine what words of praise arose from the lips of Shadrach, Meshach, and Abed-nego as they looked through the hot flames to see the God of the universe there, supporting them in their trial.

This life goal of rising up for the fame of our Lord may seem daunting at times as we evaluate our lives. It will cost us something to forsake our "little g" gods and to worship God alone. But let's not forget that He rewards those who love Him and obey His commands.

- We find joy when we partake in kingdom work because we know the end goal of experiencing eternity in the glorious presence of our Abba Father.
- There is hope to grab hold of when our eyes open to a bigger picture beyond the temporary and fleeting, and we bow low at the majestic throne of our King.
- Freedom reigns when we allow God to break the chains that take hold of our hearts and minds and keep us in fear and anxiety.

Bowing humbly before God sets us in the perfect place, with the perfect heart condition and the perfect attitude to be used by God and to fulfill our deep-seated need to make our lives matter.

Journal 2
THE ONE GOD AND OUR "LITTLE G" GODS

- ☐ Today, I would like you to to circle back to Journal 1 in this chapter, and continue to think about places in your life where you need God to teach you humility. Do you feel that you are becoming more open to taking a posture of humility before God?
- ☐ What do you think about the concept of "little g" gods? Can you honestly list some materials, people, or activities in your life on which you place more importance or attention than you do on the Lord?
- ☐ Do you see how the items on your list would steal the joy and contentment that only God can provide?
- ☐ Check out Ephesians 3:16–19 for some more encouragement on this concept. As you read it, take note of the words "fill" or "fullness" in the passage. What exactly fills us based on this scripture?

> *Father,* out of Your *honorable* and glorious riches, strengthen Your people. Fill their souls with the power of Your Spirit so that through faith the Anointed One will reside in their hearts. May love be *the rich soil* where their lives take root. May it be the bedrock where their lives are founded *so that together* with all of Your people they will have the power to understand that the love of the Anointed is infinitely long, wide, high, and deep, surpassing everything anyone previously experienced. God, may Your fullness flood through their entire beings.

Our motivation for bowing low before Jesus is based on the absolute truth that God loves us. This love is the pure fulfillment of our deepest needs, the fullness that no thing and no person on this earth can provide.

To reciprocate His love we bow low in humble awe before our King and honor Him with our words, our lives, our actions, and our thoughts.

- ☐ What is your initial reaction to the idea of experiencing God's fullness and fulfillment in life as we bow low and bask in His love?

Though God's fulfilling love is reward enough, our Father goes above and beyond to lavishly pour out blessings on those who obey His Word and present themselves with humble hearts before Him. Following are some real-life examples and wisdom from Scripture of the rewards for bowing down before the Lord. Take some time to search my Scripture references and write out the reward for bowing to God alone in each of these situations.

- ☐ Submitting to God with our romantic relationships instead of putting our boyfriends or husbands on a pedestal of perfection.

Read Ephesians 5:1–2:

> So imitate God. *Follow Him* like adored children, and live in love as the Anointed One loved you—so much that He gave Himself as a fragrant sacrifice, pleasing God.

Reward: (Example: experiencing God's perfect love that touches every space in our hearts, as no other person can)

- ☐ Submitting to God with our bank accounts; evaluating our expenditures and learning to give generously toward kingdom work, even if is a sacrifice.

Read 2 Corinthians 9:6–7:

> But I will say this *to encourage your generosity:* the one who plants little harvests little, and the one who plants plenty harvests plenty. Giving grows out of the heart—otherwise, you've reluctantly grumbled "yes" because you felt you had to or because you couldn't say "no," *but this isn't the way God wants it.* For *we know that* "God loves a cheerful giver."

Read 1 Timothy 6:10:

> For the love of money—*and what it can buy*—is the root of all sorts of evil. Some already have wandered away from the true faith because they craved what it had to offer; *but when reaching for the prize,* they found their *hands and* hearts pierced with many sorrows.

Reward: (Example: experience the exhilaration of joining God in kingdom work, finding freedom in the concept that our money is truly God's money to begin with.)

☐ Bowing low to God with our thoughts as we reject the lies of the enemy and the lies we tell ourselves. Accepting God's truth and what His Word says about our identity as lovers of Jesus.

Read 2 Corinthians 2:10 in your Bible.
Read 2 Corinthians 5:17:

> Therefore, if anyone is united with the Anointed One, that person is a new creation. The old life is gone—and see—a new life has begun!

Reward: (Example: We enjoy the blessing of our old sins washed away, forever forgotten by God as we live anew in His love.)

Your turn! Based on our running list from Journal 1 of this chapter, have you experienced any rewards from God as you bow down before Him in a particular area or situation in life? Write your answer in your journal.

RISE UP! in Prayer

Take some time to finish this prayer prompt with your own words.

- Dear Jesus, help me TODAY to place you above all else in my life because I know that You are worthy . . .
- Let Your beautiful reward of experiencing Your love and presence in my life be my ultimate motivation to bow low in these ways . . .

Check in with THE SOURCE

In an effort to share with you that God is constantly working on me personally, I'd like to get vulnerable and tell some funny and not-so-funny happenings in my life lately. These events did, in fact, humble me on the spot. Be warned, when we make the life-altering decision to RISE UP!. God roots out all kinds of junk in our hearts and minds. He purifies our motives in order to make us more effective for His kingdom purposes. Sometimes it is painful when God allows us to make blunders or allows situations to happen to us in order to humble us. Prayer is a powerful tool to take hold of as we check in with the source of wisdom, humility, mercy, grace, and love. We will never grow and learn from our mistakes and life happenings if we do not bow low in prayer before our King.

Over the past few weeks of studying and thinking and writing this very chapter, I learned to practice what I preach when it comes to humility. Here's what I wrote on Facebook that began my reflection on what God is doing in my life as I seek to RISE UP!

My Facebook status: Whew. The Lord is walking me right through what I'm presently writing about in my manuscript: dealing with my pride and putting His fame over my own name and agenda. This book is very real and raw to me. Praying it will be real, raw, and faith/life changing for those who might read it.

Here is a short rundown of a few happenings in my life lately that were a surefire way to get me on my knees in prayer asking God to pull me away from pride and toward a humble heart for His fame alone.

- I stuck my foot in my mouth in a major way in front of a crowd of fifty-plus people. I hate it when I say things that I don't mean and look like a fool.
- I experienced an amazing number of flight delays and cancellations while traveling that put a huge dent in my agenda. It really throws me off my game when my plans are rearranged.

- I neglected to put a slip on under that white summer maxi skirt in which I thought I looked super cute. And I wore the seriously see-through skirt an entire day before a good friend spoke truth to me and told me to wear proper undergarments!
- I was passed over for a really great job/ministry opportunity.

As I experienced each of these humbling events, I felt God tugging me down on my knees in prayer so I could regroup and check back in with Him, the ultimate source of wisdom and direction in my life. He was calling me back into conversation to discuss His plans, His purposes, and His desire for my heart. Though these situations were thoroughly embarrassing, life disrupting, or even heartbreaking, God used them to get me back to the habit of conversing with Him about my life and agenda. I took some intentional time to discuss life with my Jesus and soak in His presence as He calmed my heart, quelled my pride, and let me know that embarrassing myself was not the end of the world.

"God, You are great and mighty . . . I am not. I am only who I am because of You." (Isa. 41:10)

Did you notice how I said that I felt God tugging me down on my knees in prayer? This is something so very key in my personal prayer life; I literally get down on my knees to praise God in prayer. Though God and I are often having tough conversations while I pray, by taking a posture of bowing low right on my knees, I'm put in the perfect stance to receive God's truth for that moment or that season of my life. I am setting the stage to say, "God, You are great and mighty . . . I am not. I am only who I am because of You." I am reminded of God's holiness and might and even His graciousness when I release myself from the chains that weigh me down due to pride.

Additionally, when we take a literal posture of kneeling in prayer, we are showing God a heart of reverence and fear. God is ever so worthy of our bowing low before Him, both symbolically (with humbled hearts) and physically (in a kneeling posture of prayer). He doesn't need us to bow low before His throne of grace, but He is blessed when we place ourselves before His feet and join with the heavenly beings, as in Isaiah 6:3:

> "Holy, holy, holy is the LORD of hosts;
> The whole earth is full of His glory!" (NKJV)

It is when we set aside our pride and self-promotion to praise God for His holiness that He is glorified. And when we place His fame above our own, we step into a new dimension of communication with the Lord. Through prayer and conversation with the Holy One, we step out of ourselves, get over ourselves, and make much of the One that our life is all about. Then, through prayer and conversation, Jesus leads us in a life of rising up so we can make an impact on our world for His kingdom. Each time we get down on our knees and pray with humble hearts, God raises us up with His strength to do as we could never dream possible. But unless we are connected to the Source of life itself, our lives will seem meaningless, as if we are running a rat race.

Jesus is ready and willing to hear our pleas, to answer our questions. He can handle our doubts and fears.

I encourage you to look at prayer as a conversation. I think sometimes we are too intimidated by prayer, or by the feeling that we are unworthy of sitting in the presence of God, that we set it aside for another day. We don't have to be intimidated by prayer if we look at it as a reverent conversation. Jesus is ready and willing to hear our pleas, to answer our questions. He can handle our doubts and fears. He can certainly handle the sin and mistakes. Nothing we bring to Him in prayer and conversation will scare Him away.

Just come to the Lord—bowing low, ready to praise Him as holy, even if you don't feel like it.

Just come to the Lord—bowing low, ready to praise Him as holy, even if all you want to do is ask, "Why, Lord? I just don't understand."

Just come to the Lord—bowing low, ready to praise Him as holy, even if you are angry at Him.

Just come to the Lord—bowing low, ready to praise Him as holy, even if you don't feel worthy.

Just come. Just talk. Just listen. Just bow low.

By joining praise, confession of our sins, thanksgiving, and conversation as we communicate with Jesus, we open the door for the wounds of life to be healed. We allow God to set us on the right track when we've walked astray. We see life in a new light, based on the glow of God's glorious presence.

Will you bow low on your knees in prayer with me? Join me in the following journal section as we use Scripture to lead us in powerful interactive prayer. I intentionally kept my thoughts for part 3 of this chapter short so that you would have more time to dig into the following journal section. I pray you will sit for a while and experience a meaningful conversation with your Lord.

Journal 3
PRAYER JOURNALING

I hope you have been writing out your prayers in your journal as I give you the prayer prompts. By using pen and paper to journal our prayers, we are interacting with God more intentionally. How often does your mind wander as you pray? If you have a pen in hand, it keeps you more focused on the present prayer conversation with the Lord.

Let's use one of my favorite psalms (other than our Psalm 145, of course!) to interactively pray to the One who gives us life and wisdom.

In your own Bible, take a moment to read through Psalm 8. I am going to break it down into pieces using the New King James Version. After each segment, I invite you to write out your own thoughts. If this seems daunting, don't worry, I will be right there with you and will give you some starting points.

> O Lord, our Lord, How excellent is Your name in all the earth, who have set Your glory above the heavens! (v. 1)

Tell the Lord why His name is excellent. Tell Him how glorious He is in your own words.

> When I consider Your heavens, the work of Your fingers, the moon and the stars, which You have ordained, what is man that You are mindful of him, and the son of man that You visit him? (vv. 3–4)

Tell God about the beauty you see on earth that points to Him. Ask Him to show you more of His glory here on earth.

> For You have made him a little lower than the angels, And You have crowned him with glory and honor. (v. 5)

God places you and me by His side at His magnificent throne in heaven. Ask God to show you in a special way today why He thinks you are glorious in His sight.

> You have made him to have dominion over the works of Your hands; You have put all things under his feet, all sheep and oxen—even the beasts of the field, the birds of the air, and the fish of the sea that pass through the paths of the seas. (vv. 6–8)

The Lord gives us His earth to not only live in but to thrive in, with purpose. We each have a purpose here on earth as we RISE UP! Praise the Lord for allowing you to join Him in His work. Ask Him to open your eyes to see where He is leading you.

> O LORD, our Lord, how excellent is Your name in all the earth! (v. 9)

Because He is oh-so–worth it, tell Jesus one more time, in your own words, how awesome He is.

The Psalms are a great place to start to learn to pray through Scripture. I invite you now to take what you just wrote, get on your knees, and pray this psalm to the Lord one more time.

How has this journal exercise enriched your conversation with the Lord today?

Evaluate the Roadblocks, and Accept Grace and Mercy

Imagine with me that you are driving in a sleek convertible—top down, sunglasses on, hair tied back, and the fresh air invigorating your soul. This road trip is solo. It is just you, the road ahead, and your Lord. I love solo road trips because I can pick the music and sing as loud as I like. I also love solo road trips because it gives me time to think and reconnect with Jesus.

Where are you going on this road trip? What is on the horizon ahead? Go ahead . . . imagine it! Maybe this journey is one of exploration and excitement or risk as the road takes you to new and unknown places in life. Or maybe this journey is one of stepping back into your past to reconnect with memories once familiar and comfortable. Your heart sings with the possibilities of what lies ahead, and you can't help but smile as the wind whips through your hair.

Now imagine that as you drive, all of the sudden, bright orange-and-white road construction barrels pop up in the middle of the road. You almost swipe the orange barrel with your side mirror and barely miss the next as you swerve through these roadblocks. Forced to pull over, you decide to check your GPS and change course. These barrels definitely cramp your free-spirited road-trip style! They cause you to slow down and reevaluate this journey.

Are you still with me and still imagining? Good.

Let's dig in and explore what our road trip symbolizes. This exhilarating trip with the top down and wind in your hair represents your movement to RISE UP! and make Jesus famous. The excitement of the journey to get up and live differently motivates you to explore the road ahead alongside of your Lord as you worship His name and converse with Him in prayer. You intentionally chose to get behind the wheel. You decided to go down that road because you knew that staying in one place was not an option. God is moving around you, and you desire to move with Him!

Rising up is one of the thrilling possibilities on the road ahead. But sooner or later, the roadblocks—self-imposed roadblocks—of sin will stop the journey and deflate our effectiveness in our kingdom-minded mission. While we RISE UP!, we are maturing greatly in faith in so many ways. We can only continue in this matured faith if we recognize our sin and how it affects us.

Sin is anything we do, say, or think that stands in disobedience to God and His Word. The word sin is not a pretty or fun word to discuss, but it is up to us to get real and take a hard look at whether or not our actions, our words, and our thoughts please God. The fact is, each of us is sinful by nature. We live in a world that fell far from God's original plan of constant fellowship in His presence. We make personal choices daily to either walk in obedience to God, or to sin and step away from the intimate connection with the King of the universe, who loves us so dearly that He sent His son to die on the cross. When we RISE UP! we decide to accept that the blood of Jesus was shed for each and every one of us. You are not exempt from the covering of the blood of Jesus and forgiveness of your sin. Today, will you allow the blood of Christ to wash over you? Move forward on your road trip of life with a fresh start daily.

Self-imposed roadblocks of sin will stop the journey and deflate our effectiveness in our kingdom-minded mission.

It's important to address our sin because these self-imposed roadblocks . . .

- separate us from an intimate connection with Jesus. God is pure and holy. Our sin blocks us from God's crystal clear, clean, beautiful, refreshing presence.
- separate us from God's plan for our lives. When we live for earthly pleasures, we are standing against God's desires and commands.

- separate us from God's light. Sin keeps us in dark places in our hearts and sometimes even in the world around us. We were not meant to live in darkness.

> But you are a chosen people, *set aside to be* a royal order of priests, a holy nation, God's own; so that you may proclaim the wondrous acts of the One who called you out of *inky* darkness into shimmering light. (1 Peter 2:9)

You are God's own. You were chosen for this moment, this time, to live in His shimmering light and let your world know about it. The inky darkness is pervasive in this world. But it is God's marvelous light that brings us into clear life purpose as we look toward Him and live as His holy people . . . making a big impact on the inky-dark world around us in God's power and with His ultimate direction.

But it is God's marvelous light that brings us into clear life purpose as we look toward Him and live as His holy people.

Our concept of humbly bowing low before God plays into this as well. Much of our rising up is an outward expression as we live lives of praise and do life differently. But this aspect of rising up, the act of bowing low and dealing with our sin, is a decision that starts with quiet moments with God in prayer and confession. Asking God to reveal the dark areas of our lives is asking Him a loaded question. We must be ready for Him to root out places in our lives that we might not be ready to revamp. It may even hurt sometimes when we are asked to confess sins that are fun or pleasurable at the moment but in the end do not please God.

The other day I was tending to my "garden." I put that word garden in quotes because it really isn't a garden but a bunch of potted plants neatly arranged on my front porch. It is the best I can do with my lack of knowledge of perennials, annuals, fertilizer, and sunlight. I sat on the brick steps, chatting with my mom on the phone while I plucked out dead petals (there were many, I tell you!) from a pretty, pink plant. Don't ask me what the name of the plant is, but it's a shade of hot pink that makes me smile, so that's all that matters in my book.

As I was mindlessly plucking, I accidentally plucked a fresh, good bud from the plant. My not-so-careful pruning skills haphazardly ravaged this plant, and I did more harm than good. Let us rest assured that God, the ever-caring Gardener who knows our names and the desires of our hearts, prunes His own with careful hands. He snips and cuts back the gardens of our souls to allow us to grow and become more like Jesus.

The following is a descriptive and beautiful illustration for us to look to when examining our lives, our sin, and our relationship to Jesus. Here we see that God, the Vine Keeper, keeps a close hand on those who are His. He desires for us to live in His fullness instead of the emptiness in which sin pulls us.

> I am the true vine, and My Father is the keeper of the vineyard. My Father examines every branch in Me and cuts away those who do not bear fruit. He leaves those bearing fruit and carefully prunes them so that they will bear more fruit; already you are clean because you have heard My voice. Abide in Me, and I will abide in you. A branch cannot bear fruit if it is disconnected from the vine, and neither will you if you are not connected to Me. (John 15:1–4)

If we come before our Lord with hearts ready to take a hard look at our sin, He cuts out sin like anger, jealousy, sexual immorality, and greed. When we present our lives as gardens before the pruning shears of the Ultimate Gardener, He prunes and cuts back ugly spaces in our hearts and minds that separate us from continual connection. We need this connection with Jesus. We must have it if we are to thrive in a way that is not just talk or placard statements but true kingdom actions and lifestyles.

I'd like to bring in a very biblical word that is often looked at in a negative manner: repentance. It is crucial that we confess our sins to God. The next crucial step is to take action to leave that particular sin behind and change our thoughts and actions. It is not always pleasant to make tough decisions to step away—no, cut away the sin-filled areas of our lives. At the moment, sins seemingly provide pleasure or gratification. For example, today I received an e-mail that critiqued a blog I recently wrote. I felt a bit blasted and misunderstood. I got angry and was tempted to shoot back an ugly response. My heart pumped fiery rage through my veins. But after I calmed down, the Lord reminded me of my own sin in this matter. He opened my eyes to my quick temper. Honestly, I didn't want to calm down. At the moment, it was much more gratifying to feel the anger course through my veins and fester in my heart. But deeper down, I knew this attitude was not pleasing to God. Repentance for me in this instance was to step away from the anger and address the sender with respect. If I had moved forward in rage, I would have stepped away from a sense of peace and joy that God promises. Great reward comes our way when we confess sin and repent—that is, change our ways.

"I am the vine, and you are the branches. If you abide in Me and I in you, you will bear great fruit. Without Me, you will accomplish nothing." (John 15:5)

John 15 talks much about fruit. If sin separates us from Jesus, the flip side is that repentance and obedience (sticking close to Him) produces fruit in our lives, namely, the fruit of the Spirit that Paul wrote about in Galatians 5. When we step away from sin, redirect our course in repentance, and stay connected with the Lord, He promises love, joy, peace, patience, kindheartedness, goodness, faithfulness, gentleness, and self-control. Each of these molds our hearts to live more like Jesus. Each fruit adds depth to our personal character as we live out our faith and love for our King. When we "taste" this fruit daily and allow God to enrich it in our lives, we then see that fruit grow in more of an outward expression. Those around us see the fruit and want some for themselves. Our actions may even encourage them to examine their lives, repent, abide in Christ, and RISE UP! to pluck their own fruit off the tree, so to speak.

It is my hope that you will take a posture of bowing low before your King with a humble heart in confession of sin. But let's not stop there; let's repent and really do life differently. As one who has sinned much in the past and who struggles with sin daily, I want to encourage you that God doesn't waste anything, not even our sin. There are many times in my life when, after I've repented and changed my ways, God uses the lessons learned from mistakes and sins as ministry to others. (Remember, we don't have to be preachers to do ministry!) I can relate to those who are hurting because of their sin because I have walked in their shoes. But now I can share how God, the ever-caring Gardener, has pruned me and cut away the sin so I can live in His glorious light, bearing much fruit. Hurting people in our lives desperately need to hear of God's mercy and forgiveness of sins. They need to hear that with repentance comes great fruit. Please don't allow your feelings of guilt over sin to keep you from rising up. Christ paid the price. Once and for all. It is your choice now to hold tight to that forgiveness and to allow your life to reflect His amazing grace. Make Jesus famous by sharing, unabashedly, how He personally impacts your life and your heart.

From here on out let us not allow ourselves to feel disqualified from rising up because of our past sin. If you come before Jesus, presenting Him with a heart repentant and ready to change, eager to RISE UP!, you are qualified, my friend. The grace that Jesus pours out freely is a gift He wrapped with you in mind. He tied the bow on this beautiful present and handed it over to you to unwrap, try on, live in, and live out. Take the gift of grace today and praise your King; then pass along the gift by making His name famous in your world.

Join me in the following journal segment as we examine our self-imposed roadblocks. Let's get real, let's repent, and let's RISE UP!

Journal 4
EVALUATE THE ROADBLOCKS AND ACCEPT GRACE AND MERCY

I wonder if the word sin makes you want to shut this book and never return to the pages. It's okay. Sin is not a pretty word. But now I want to pitch out two absolutely beautiful words: grace and mercy.

Take a quick minute to jot down your own definition of these two words. What comes to mind first when you see *grace*? *mercy*?

These two beautiful words are heavy with meaning for us personally. In a few words, grace and mercy are the free gifts God gives to forgive our sins through the blood Jesus shed on the cross.

> The Eternal is gracious.
> He shows mercy to *His people*.
> *For Him* anger does not come easily, but faithful love does—
> and it is *rich and* abundant.
> But the Eternal's goodness *is not exclusive*—it is offered *freely*
> to all.
> His mercy extends to all His creation. (Ps. 145:8–9)

- [ ] Based on this scripture, how do you feel about the free gift of grace, mercy, and forgiveness of sins? Do you have a hard time accepting this gift? If so, why?

Now couple the verses from Psalm 145 with 2 Corinthians 5:17–18:

> Therefore, if anyone is united with the Anointed One, that person is a new creation. The old life is gone—and see—a new life has begun! All of this is a *gift* from *our* Creator God, who has pursued us and brought us into a restored *and healthy* relationship with Him through the Anointed. And He has given us *the same mission,* the ministry of reconciliation, *to bring others back to Him.*

Each day we have a new opportunity to accept the collective gift of grace, mercy, and forgiveness and step into the truth that we are a new creation. This free gift is so glorious that it should motivate us strongly to evaluate our sins daily. Take some time right now to get on your knees in conversation with Jesus about your recent sin. Hand it over to Him and allow Him to hand over His grace, mercy, and forgiveness to you.

Here is where the rubber meets the road. After you've evaluated your sin, how will you repent and live differently? I think the biggest motivation for repentance and change is living in the reality that we can have a personal relationship with Jesus. When we make our faith personal, when we really talk to Him, when we converse with Jesus as if He is a real person in our lives rather than a figure in heaven, we begin to live to please Him because He is worthy. It becomes more than checking the box and saying, "Nope, didn't do that sin today. I'm good to go." We begin to desire to be more like Him, and to praise Him with our entire lives out of reverence and commitment.

Each day we have a new opportunity to accept the collective gift of grace, mercy, and forgiveness and step into the truth that we are a new creation.

Let's approach our Lord at His throne with our sin and willingness to accept His gift of grace, mercy, and forgiveness. Then, let's change the way we live. Use the following prompts to start a conversation with Jesus. Allow Him to show you your roadblocks and illuminate the dark places. Then allow Him to work in you and through you to produce fruit so you can go and live out your faith and RISE UP!

Fill in your thoughts and prayers in the space following each prayer prompt.

- Father God, show me the areas in my life that are sinful and not pleasing to you . . .

- Make my heart more willing to hand this sin over to You . . .
- Lord, I accept Your gift of grace, mercy, and forgiveness because I know . . .
- These are ways that I commit to you in repentance as I change and live my life to please You . .
- I know I can only repent and change in Your strength . . .

☐ How does it feel to take your sin to the Lord in confession, repentance, and in conversation with Him?

Thank you for taking time to get real and get raw about sin. The more we do this, the more we recognize where we fall short and where He is glorious and merciful. I pray that a transformation will happen in your life as you daily talk to Jesus about the not-so-pretty stuff (like sin) and then allow Him to make that conversation beautiful as you grow closer and more like Jesus.

Do Life Differently: Gather Your Armor

Two years ago the Lord placed this RISE UP! concept on my heart as a rally cry to encourage my blog readers to do life differently: to make their lives count for something, to make Jesus famous in the process, and to lead others to do the same. It was a concept near and dear to my heart as I worked to practice what I preached for myself. A game changer. This past new year, I sat quietly before Jesus with a restless heart. I felt a bit off-kilter, like a little gopher popping up my head above ground, peeking to see what everyone else was doing. I wanted to keep up with my friends (both online and offline). I wanted to be sure I was in the know, and my head spun with too much information at my fingertips. Coupled with my excitement for the RISE UP! theme in my life, I felt a new layer of a life theme forming: pursue the presence of God. That was my goal, to daily soak in His presence, keep my focus on Him alone, and be sensitive to His Holy Spirit.

> Come close to the one true God, and He will draw close to you. Wash your hands; you have dirtied them in sin. Cleanse your heart, because your mind is split down the middle, *your love for God on one side and selfish pursuits on the other.* (James 4:8)

This pursuit of God's presence is like a soft blanket and a cup of hot tea on a cold winter day. When life gets crazy and I'm tempted to pop my head up just to keep up, He covers me with His warm presence and calms my spirit. I am then refreshed and revitalized and refocused on Him. This is my prayer for you too—that you will accept the promise straight from Scripture that when you pursue God, when you draw near to Him, He will be found. We have discussed so many aspects of this pursuit already in this chapter. Through prayer and worship, we pursue His presence and guidance. He speaks to our deepest needs. By reading His Scripture daily, we connect with His commands that are for our good, that make us more effective in His kingdom. When we pursue God with repentant hearts, we rid ourselves of sin and please Him with our thoughts, words, and actions. We are doing life differently as we make choices in our day to focus on Him instead of our selfish pursuits. We must bow low at His throne, and He will draw us even closer to Him.

Here's where things get interesting. When we make the life-altering decision to RISE UP!—to get real about the self-imposed roadblocks of sin, to bow low before the King alone, and to live our lives full of praise and with kingdom perspective—we become dangerous. Yes, dangerous. Not a threat to the people around us, for they need to see Jesus famous in our lives. Rather, we are dangerous to the devil. The enemy despises anyone and everyone who chooses to make the King known in this world, which so desperately needs to hear of His love, His truth, His greatness. The enemy of God is, in fact, a mighty fighter. God allows the devil to have His way in this world. Hear me say, though, that God's enemy is not greater than our King. Satan is only allowed to have his way for a time before God releases His full might and power to once and for all defeat him. We know the end of the story; we know that the devil will lose. In the meantime, will we choose to fight the battle alongside our King, to do our part to make Him famous and bring others along with us to do the same?

When you pursue God, when you draw near to Him, He will be found.

Good news: God gives us all the weapons we need to fight this battle against the enemy. This is a very real battle that calls for powerful women (like us!) to decide to pick up the weapons, relying on God's strength and not our own. It takes us getting on our knees daily with humble hearts as God equips us with all that we need to fight the enemy. Ephesians 6 spells out this battle and lists the powerful armor that we must utilize. Let's not shy away from the truth that the enemy prowls around ready to discourage us from our mission of rising up . . .

> Finally, *brothers and sisters,* draw your strength and might from God. Put on the full armor of God to protect yourselves from the devil and his evil schemes. We're not waging war against enemies of flesh and blood alone. No, this fight is against tyrants, against authorities, against *supernatural* powers and *demon princes that slither* in the darkness of this world, and against wicked *spiritual armies* that lurk about in heavenly places. (Eph. 6:10–12)

It may seem that we constantly battle the opinions of others, maybe even their ridicule, when we choose to live differently. We must realize that our enemy is more serious than people who look to tear us down because they don't understand our need to pursue God. Our enemy is dark and powerful, but we have a mighty God who will overcome that darkness. We have the chance to fight alongside our King and experience for ourselves His grandeur and might. We have the opportunity to see God's kingdom at hand, to see lives changed and restored when we put on the armor of God and RISE UP!

Let's read further in Ephesians 6 as the author, Paul, lists out the armor of God that is available for the taking should we decide to join in the battle. I love the idea that we are all soldiers in this battle with the enemy. This war is one worth fighting. We are daily assaulted with unhealthy images in our world that distract us from knowing we are beautiful in God's eyes. Our families are threatened as the enemy looks to break up marriages and tear apart loved ones. Our friends suffer from the enemy's darkness because they don't know the one true God, who is full of hope and light. This is not a time to shy away from the battle. Will you join me? Lace up your combat boots (mine are pink, of course!), and put on the powerful armor of God.

> And this is why you need *to be head-to-toe in* the full armor of God: so you can resist during these evil days and be fully prepared to hold your ground. (v.13)

God promises to protect and arm us head to toe. The devil won't find a chink in our armor when we are wearing what God provides.

> Yes, stand—truth banded around your waist, righteousness as your chest plate. (v. 14)

The belt of truth holds all the other tools of God's armor and reminds us to stand ready to live our lives in the truth of God and not sway back and forth with the lies of the enemy. The chest plate of righteousness protects our most vulnerable area, our hearts. As we put on the righteousness we find in Christ, we stand against the temptation of sin and live our lives more like Jesus.

> and feet protected in preparation to proclaim the good news of peace. (v. 15)

This is where the combat boots come in! Lace up the boots and be ready to walk on the firm foundation of God's kingdom that will not be shaken. May we lead others to the kingdom as we walk with a sure footing because we know God's truth.

> Don't forget to raise the shield of faith above all else, so you will be able to extinguish flaming spears hurled at you from the wicked one. (v. 16)

Raising this shield of faith is a daily, even minute-by-minute decision to deflect the temptations from the enemy. He will try ever so hard to make us ineffective in God's kingdom due to our sin. Resist!

> Take also the helmet of salvation and the sword of the Spirit, which is the word of God. (v. 17)

The helmet of salvation is the assurance that you are God's child when you live for Jesus alone. Though the enemy will try to tempt you elsewhere, nothing will change your standing with God. He will never leave you nor forsake you! (Heb. 13:5 NKJV)

Oh, friends, let us pick up the ever-powerful, ever-sharp sword of the Spirit, God's Holy Word. By reading and rehearsing truth every day, we won't allow the enemy to feed us lies to distract us from rising up.

> Pray always. Pray in the Spirit. Pray about everything in every way you know how! (v. 18a)

This is the way we stay connected to our ultimate source of truth. We must plug in and converse with the Lord continually through our day to find assurance, to find forgiveness, to find hope, to find joy, to find peace, to find a firm foundation.

This enemy of ours is ready to rock our world and keep us from making the name of Jesus famous to those around us. He knows we are armed and dangerous, so let's not disappoint the enemy with a weak, apathetic fight. No! Let's take up our armor and go to battle ready for the victory already proclaimed in God's Word, all the while encouraging others with God's hope and light as we RISE UP!

Journal 5
DO LIFE DIFFERENTLY: GATHER YOUR ARMOR

That last section was a lot to digest. Take a moment to think about this battle we talked about.

- ☐ How do you see the battle waging in your own life? What tricks and darts does the enemy tend to throw your way?
- ☐ How do you see the armor of God as a powerful way to fight the battle?

Check back in with Psalm 145 in your journal. Take some time to write out a verse or two that encourages you to RISE UP! and join God in the spiritual battle.

As we close this chapter, be sure to circle back to Journal 1 and keep evaluating ways in your life that God is leading you to bow low and serve Him with a humble heart.

Notes

Notes

CHAPTER FOUR

OUR Dreams, Purpose, AND God's Agenda

Throughout this book you will hear me say that you don't have to be a preacher, an author, or someone with a PhD in divinity to do ministry. Every day we have the opportunity to minister with our lives if we surrender to God's leading. I firmly believe there is a desire within the hearts of women to make a difference with our lives, yet we don't always know how. The key is to allow God to do big things in our lives by seeking after Him instead of just seeking after a dream or a passion. Dreams and passions are good, but they are most effective if God is the one who plants and nurtures them in our lives.

We will explore this more in this chapter, but first I want to share a moment with you that I had while working on this book. I share this moment because when we decide to RISE UP! and allow the Lord to do big things in our lives, it may be tempting to allow insecurity to have its way and dampen our God-given passion.

I typed this one day on Facebook during a trip to visit my family in Texas . . .

> Writing morning here in Texas. The other day I wanted to just throw up my hands in surrender. To just shut it all down and not write or speak another "ministry" word and go hide away in a pretty farmhouse in Central Texas—letting the wildflowers speak to my soul. I wanted to just escape because this is tough. I feel like I don't measure up. Like it doesn't really matter what I write or what I speak.
>
> But, the fact is, this is my passion. My God-given passion. If I didn't do what I am blessed to do everyday, if I just escaped, sooner or later that need to type, that need to "do ministry," would well up again.

We all have an opportunity to seek out our God-given passion. We ALL have chances everyday to "do ministry" in the way we love God and love others. It is hard, though. It hurts sometimes to put ourselves out there and be vulnerable. But if we are doing what only God could plant in our hearts to do . . . there is no escaping it.

Will you seek out your God-given passion today with abandonment . . . with an open heart (protected by the Almighty) and do life . . . do ministry?

I invite you to join me in a conversation with my friend Lindsay. Lindsay is a professional event planner who, with in the past several years, decided to RISE UP! and follow Jesus by surrendering her life, her dreams, and her own agenda to Him alone. Lindsay is one of those women who can't help but point me to Jesus because her whole life reflects that of someone who desires Him and His presence above all.

SARAH Lindsay, I can't wait to get your take. What are your thoughts on the concept of rising up and making Jesus famous?

LINDSAY When I think of this challenge to RISE UP! and make Jesus famous, I think that is exactly what He wants us to do with our whole life. I also think it can be done in so many more ways than we can even wrap our minds around. The Lord designed each and every one of us uniquely and put a dream in our hearts that is attached to His agenda for this world, and I believe it all leads to that very phrase—battle cry, if you will—"Making Jesus Famous!"

SARAH So, how do you negotiate the difference between our personal agenda—things we dream about doing—and God's ultimate plan? How do you align the two?

LINDSAY That's honestly a hard question. I think for me, not knowing Jesus for thirty-one years of my life, I struggled to know God's heart, His plan, for me. I sense it is so very important to know God's heart for you and allow yourself to receive His love and adoration. It is only after receiving this that we can join in on His agenda. The interesting part was, once I was able to fully receive His love, I was able to trust Him to lead me to His agenda, through my dream, a dream He placed in me.

SARAH Wow, Lindsay. Sounds like you have been on a journey with God as He reveals His plan for you and births dreams and purpose in your heart.

LINDSAY Oh yes, totally. It was through anguish that this was all birthed. Jesus came and rescued me from extreme heartache with a sweet kiss on my forehead. It was honestly as weird as it sounds, but my heart melted, and I believe it was then pliable enough for Him to do what He wanted in and through me.

Lindsay shared with me how heartache from a broken romantic relationship put her in a vulnerable position before the Lord. Have you ever been in a place where everything around you seems so dark and dismal, as if there's no hope or happiness for you? God often uses these times to call us back into His loving arms. Lindsay described it as she "couldn't see straight and felt isolated and rejected." The only thing she could think to do was sit with Jesus. And just as our loving Father does, He mended her heart and reminded her of a dream He had placed in her heart before she even knew God at all. As a little girl, Lindsay had dreamed of writing and using her words to touch people, to make a difference in their lives. "The dream He put in me lined up with His heart for others, His agenda," she said. "I know only a perfect God could or would do that."

We can be our own worst enemy when it comes to insecurity and allow that to block us from living out the calling God places on our life.

As God healed Lindsay's heart and brought her into His light, out of rejection and isolation, Lindsay began to write, to string words together, knowing that she must follow her God-given dream. Step-by-step, as she stuck close to Jesus and sought after Him, God confirmed this dream and passion to write with exciting opportunities to share her words with others. After a while Lindsay began to experience some doubt about her calling toward ministry in writing. She says the enemy didn't let up in his quest to tempt her with guilt. It felt as if the enemy was saying, "Lindsay, writing doesn't help anyone. You need to go house the homeless people, rescue girls out of sex trafficking. If you just sit here and write and think that is helping anyone, you are so selfish, Lindsay." Thank goodness, Lindsay learned quickly that the devil is a liar!

That is an important lesson: to call the devil out. It is also extremely important to call out our own insecurity as we pursue God's dreams and purpose for our lives. We can be our own worst enemy when it comes to insecurity and allow that to block us from living out the calling God places on our life.

As we mature and grow in our faith, it is so crucial to develop a yearning to hear God's voice and ignore the voices that tell us we are not worthy of serving God almighty. When we do hear His voice (through reading His Word, the Bible, and through prayer), it is exciting, but sometimes He asks us to make tough choices in order to follow His voice and leading.

Will we be ever so focused in making Jesus famous that we choose Jesus, or will we cave and do what is safe and comfortable? Will we be bold and brave even if it means we must take a giant step outside our safe and cozy comfort zone?

Throughout this chapter, I hope that you will be motivated to seek out God Himself rather than a personal dream or agenda. What if we asked these questions of ourselves at the end of each day:

- Did I seek out Jesus and desire His presence today?
- Do I want to know the heart of the King of the universe more than I want the desires of my own flawed, self-focused heart?
- Do I want God to do big things in my life and through my life, or do I seek out my own plan, my own path, my own fame?

Journal 1

OUR DREAMS, PURPOSE, AND GOD'S AGENDA

In the opening paragraph of this chapter I said, "The key is to allow God to do big things in our lives by seeking after Him instead of just seeking after a dream or a passion. Dreams and passions are good things, but they are most effective if God is the one who plants and nurtures them in our lives."

- ☐ Do you feel as if you are searching or seeking for passion or purpose or a dream in your life these days? If so, what does that search look like daily? Are you finding fulfillment? Are you always trying new things to pinpoint exactly what gives you passion or purpose?
- ☐ What are your thoughts on my quote from the opening paragraph of this chapter?
- ☐ Lindsay talks about how God used a breakup with her boyfriend to make her heart more pliable and ready to be used for God's plans. Do you think your heart is pliable? If so, what got you to that point? If not, go ahead and pray for God to work through this and make you ready for His plans and purposes.

Take a moment to touch base with our home scripture of Psalm 145. In this chapter we will hone in on verses 15–19. Please read them and write one verse (or more!) that speaks to you from this chapter. What about that verse catches your attention?

RISE UP! in Prayer

Take some time to finish these prayer prompts with your own words on the pages of your journal.

- Father God, I want so badly to have a purpose and a plan in my life. Help me to seek You first . . .
- Lord, thank You for the talents and gifts You created in me. Help me to use the talents for Your fame . . .
- Make my heart pliable, Lord . . .

RISE UP! In Expectation

I remember the exact moment when my faith and my entire life collided into a clear focus. I sat in my favorite red chair with my comfy blanket and a cup of hot tea as I snuggled in with my Bible and a new book. The book was huge, several hundred pages long, and yet it didn't intimidate me one bit. It will stay on my favorite book list forever. Written by the beloved Chuck Colson, *How Now Shall We Live?* set the lens of life in focus so that I now include my faith in every square inch of my existence. For years I struggled with this imbalance of my faith in one hand and the rest of my life in the other hand. This book spelled out this segregation for me and challenged me to place my King, Jesus, in the center of my entire life—not leaving Him out of anything. This game changer also challenged me to not sit idle but to go and tell others all about what God had just downloaded into my life.

What happened next was a bit uncharacteristic of me as a type A personality who loves to jump in with both feet. You see, when I get passionate about something, all I want is to engulf myself in that something. This time was different, though, as God calmed my passionate spirit and drew me into a time of waiting, learning, reading of His Word, praying, and just soaking in His presence. I think I obeyed instead of jumping into some sort of project to spread the word out of sheer bliss that I now could make sense of my life, my faith, and how the two are intricately woven together. This sweet time of waiting lasted several months, and I look back at the time with fondness.

I wonder if, as you have turned the pages of this book, you have cultivated the desire to find purpose or a dream or a project—something to live out what has been planted in your heart to make Jesus famous. I hope you said yes! I am right there with you, friend, cheering for you. Maybe . . .

- you have thoughts about leading a Bible study to share your passion of making Jesus famous

- you are thinking through some sort of mission project overseas
- you see the need in your own backyard (your community), and you want to do something about it in the name of your King Jesus
- you are contemplating how you will voice this newfound passion to RISE UP! and tell others about it

I encourage you to take some time to wait in expectation for the what and the how and the when of these dreams and purposes that God is planting in your heart. This itch, this desire to do something meaningful with our lives, shouldn't outweigh or override our passion for seeking God's presence. A heart full of worship spills into an openness to receive God's call. Let's seek Him first, then chase after the actions we must take to live out our passionate faith.

Join me back in Psalm 145 as we allow God's Word to call us into a time of seeking Him.

> All eyes have turned toward You, *waiting in expectation; when they are hungry,* You feed them right on time. (v. 15)

I believe that as we have practiced a life of worship and kingdom perspective, our eyes have, in fact, turned toward our Jesus. During the rising up, we can't help but look up toward heaven. Our perspectives have matured to see Him as the One who is worthy of all praise and adoration. Verse 15 of Psalm 145 reminds us to continue a steadfast focus on Him even through life's drama and distractions that threaten our consistent and constant praise of Jesus. As we seek Him for our dreams and purpose in life, let's remember that what we consume through our eyes affects the condition of our hearts. The more we soak in God's presence daily and spend time with Him, the more our hearts are molded and conformed to His image—the image of Jesus. We become more like Him; we train our eyes, our hearts, and our minds to seek after the Lord above all else.

Something interesting will also happen in this holy seeking to be more like Jesus. We will realize that there are elements in our lives that aren't pleasing to Him and aren't as fulfilling to us as we once thought they were. When we live differently, we pinpoint things that we consume with our eyes that dull the passion to seek after God and maybe even muddy our hearts away from a pure life. These muddy elements are different for everyone, but the commonality for all of us is that they keep us looking to the right and to the left in distraction instead of looking up toward our holy King. The wonderful news is that once we spend more and more time in the presence of God through prayer, worship, and the Word, God will show us in very personal ways how He is so much greater than what once distracted us from a clear focus on Him.

Waiting in expectation. Doesn't that phrase just put you in a place of curiosity about what God will do? I love the word expectation, as it drums up excitement and even mystery. Of course, our ultimate fulfillment of expectation is seeing our Jesus in full glory and majesty when we set our eyes on Him in person one day. Whenever I'm having a blah kind of day regarding my faith, whenever I need something to look forward to when I've had a stressful day, it helps to sit and close my eyes and imagine the great day when I will see Jesus in person. This creates a sense of expectation and excitement as I ask myself . . .

- What will He look like?
- What colors will surround His glorious presence?
- What sounds of worship will fill my ears that I've never experienced before?
- What will I do in worship of Him?

This forward-looking expectation of seeing the King face-to-face can fuel our passion of expectation of what He will do in our lives in the meantime. There is work to be done in the kingdom. But before we jump into kingdom work, we must:

- wait for God to plant and nurture this work He has for us
- wait for Him to lay the path we must walk on as we make the name of Jesus famous in our world
- wait in His Word for ultimate wisdom
- wait in prayer as God speaks to our hearts and heals wounds that might hamper us

We know that our waiting is not in vain, based on our reading of the second part of Psalm 145:15.

> When they are hungry, You feed them right on time.

Does God meet our physical hunger, our physical needs? Absolutely. At the same time, again and again in the Bible, God shows us that our spiritual hunger, our heart condition, is of higher priority to Him than our physical needs. When tempted in the desert by the devil during a forty-day fast, Jesus made the bold declaration straight from Scripture that "man does not live by bread alone. Rather, he lives on every word that comes from the mouth of the Eternal One" (Matt. 4:4). God's Word is transformational and will impact every square inch of our lives if we allow it.

If we are honest, though, sometimes we don't have a hunger for God's Word or a desire for His presence. Sometimes it comes down to the fact that we don't know how or we just don't feel like enjoying God Himself. I propose a simple, yet loaded prayer as we go straight to the source of our delight in Him.

Father God, give us eyes to look past ourselves and see Your beauty bountiful in the world surrounding us. Help us to clear away the cobwebs that dampen the brightness of Your presence that already surrounds us. Give us hearts full of worship of Your glory. Help us to wait in expectation and enjoy You, O God. Amen!

Some other words that come to mind when I think of enjoyment and expectation:

- Relish. May we taste Your goodness as we actively pursue You day by day. May we see and relish Your zest and spice in life as we look past our so-called mundane activities. For it is in the mundane that we find comfort and security, but Lord! let us see Your spice of life in our routine and mandatory to-do lists.
- Delight. Give us a twinkle in our eyes as we think of You as our Father, our King, and our Friend. May we delight in new and fresh conversations with You throughout our days. Show us what You delight in, Lord. Stretch our hearts toward delighting in those things too.
- Savor. Help us to slow down and soak in your presence, savoring our moments with You. Remind us that Your presence is ever-fulfilling and satisfying—the ultimate blessing.

It is our choice, daily, to enjoy Him, to relish and actively pursue Him, to delight in His friendship, to savor His presence. It is our choice to simply ask Him to give us a fresh perspective and a heart willing to enjoy Him. By living a life of worship, looking to enjoy God and waiting in expectation, we develop this fresh perspective and live outside of ourselves to look toward His grandeur. For it is by standing in that grandeur (rather than our own plans and agendas) that our souls delight, relish, savor, and enjoy the place where God has us right here and now.

"You feed them right on time" (Ps. 145:15). This is a promise straight from Scripture and one we can stand firm on as we wait for God to lay out His plan and purpose. Earlier in our conversation, we discussed the Lord's Prayer, where Jesus taught His disciples to ask God to "give us this day our daily bread" (Matt. 6:11 NKJV). Yes, of course, God provides for our physical hunger, but I want to circle back to the spiritual hunger. As we wait expectantly in God's presence daily, as we worship and pray and ask to be filled up with His Holy Spirit, God promises that He will give us exactly what we need to do life today, in the here and now. When I get overwhelmed with ideas, projects, ministry, and passions, I'm tempted to drown in too many details of the how, the what, and the when. I wonder if you, too, feel overwhelmed with our mission to RISE UP! Over the years I've found peace by asking God this one question when it comes to my daily purpose . . .

Lord, what is the ONE THING You want me to do today to make Your name famous?

This question, coupled with a heart to wait in expectation, will put us in a position to receive what God has for us (our daily bread) for that day. He is always right on time. Our God is so gracious to pour out His presence and more of Himself upon those who are hungry for Him above all else. When the question, "What do You want me to do with my life?" swirls in our hearts, God promises to bless us with the desires of our heart. Join me in the following journal section as we dig a bit more into the concept of the desires of our hearts and how we align them with God's plan and purposes.

Journal 2
WAITING IN EXPECTATION

- ☐ Let's continue together working through Psalm 145 and add verse 16 to our discussion of waiting in expectation and seeking God in our lives:

  > The desires of every living thing are met by Your open hand.

- ☐ I love comparing scripture with scripture. Let's couple Psalm 145:16 with Psalm 37. Both of these passages talk about God providing for our desires. In your Bible read Psalm 37:3–4. Take a moment to write out those two verses in your journal.
- ☐ This passage in Psalm 37 reminds us that God will give us the desires of our hearts if . . . What is the "if" in this verse?
- ☐ Do you think our desires and passions and dreams will transform and evolve when we delight in the Lord and wait expectantly? If so, how? Why do you think this is key in rising up to make Jesus famous?
- ☐ How can you delight in the Lord today as you wait in His presence?

RISE UP! in Prayer

Take some time to finish this prayer prompt with your own words in the pages of your journal.

- Father, give me the patience to sit still and wait with expectation for what You have for my life . . .
- Show me, Lord, in a personal way what it means to delight in You alone . . .

The Righteous Road Trip

Can I take a moment to vent a bit with you? I get frustrated with some of the images posted on social media. I'm talking about images with pretty fonts and motivational phrases that contain flat statements such as "Dream Big!," "IMAGINE!," or "Just Believe!" Visually they are interesting and maybe a bit motivating. Please know that I've done my fair share of Pinterest pinning and reposting of graphics that inspire and point to God's truth with Bible verses and neat images. In fact, I make a lot of them myself to share with my friends. It is fun to read these inspirational images online and view them in greeting cards or wall plaques. Even so, as we RISE UP!, I encourage you to rise beyond flat motivational statements as you navigate and pray through where God is taking you in life.

> **I encourage you to rise beyond flat motivational statements as you navigate and pray through where God is taking you in life.**

When we cling to the "dream big" or "just imagine" motivational phrases, we just might be clinging to an emotion that those phrases conjure up instead of clinging to the ever-big God that has ever-big things to do in our lives when we follow Him and His plan for us. I find the "dream big" mentality to be flat and more of a self-help mantra than a call to seek after God for direction. This flat thought process often leads to that adrenaline rush of excitement that may steer us toward our own journey in life instead of the most meaningful journey we should take, the one God lays out for us. My friend Shari reminded me of an important fact regarding clinging to motivational thought processes such as dream big. She said, "By just dreaming big we might cling to a false foundation rather than seeking our true foundation—His Word! These flat statements don't display God promises laid out in the Bible for those who love and obey Him; they don't encourage a relationship with Jesus."

One of these promises for us in Scripture lies in our home base of Psalm 145:

> The Eternal is right in all His ways, and He is kind in all His acts. (v. 17)

I would like for us to circle back to the analogy of the road trip that we conversed about in chapter 3. Let's think again about the sleek convertible and our hair pulled back and the wind in our faces. If we allow Jesus into every square inch our lives, this journey of rising up should naturally converge with whatever season of life we are in at the moment. We are the most successful (in kingdom economy) and most personally fulfilled when we allow God to work in us and use us. We have purpose.

This feeling of purpose and fulfillment starts with our willingness to join God in His plan and allow Him to navigate our life road trip. In Psalm 145:17 we see that God, the Eternal, is right in all His ways. The Hebrew word for "ways" is derek (pronounced deh'-rek) and the definition for the word way contains phrases such as

- a road
- a figurative course of life or mode of action

By aligning our hearts with God's and molding our desires to fit with His plan, we are joining Him on His road, His plan, His course of action for His Kingdom. Lest we think this only applies to acts of ministry and service of others within the church setting, let's make sure to apply the concept of God's ways (derek) in every part of our lives. Earlier on in our conversation I asked you to think about where this road trip you are on is taking you. What journey are you presently on?

Are you . . .

- seeking out a new career and desperate to figure out what you are passionate about and can also get paid for?

- working through a new family dynamic and finding your personal role in it?
- striving to pay off debt and learning how to manage not only money itself but your personal expectations of how money (or the lack thereof) affects you and your search for personal fulfillment?
- in a new romantic relationship, figuring out how to balance your passionate feelings for this man with your strong desire to obey and please God with your relationship?
- in a new phase of marriage where life isn't a honeymoon anymore as you learn what it means to love "for better or for worse"?

I propose that as we are all on our individual road trips that God has intricately laid out for us, let us embrace this time and look forward down the road ahead. All too often it is tempting to veer off the road and create our own path because we don't understand why God has us where we are at this very moment. Isn't it also tempting to rubberneck and look over to the other lane to observe what others are doing—sometimes in pure jealousy for what we see as a "better" path? Don't we frequently think we know better than God what road we should be taking, what exit we should choose and what lane we should drive in? But, if we truly desire to RISE UP! and embrace our specific life journeys, we have to wrap our self-focused minds around the fact that God's ways are right. Some translations of Psalm 145:17 use the word "righteous." This word is not only defined as "morally just or virtuous," but it is also used to describe an act that is perfectly wonderful and genuine.[1]

It is tempting to veer off the road and create our own path because we don't understand why God has us where we are at this very moment.

We are not at risk of missing out on the genuine, perfect ways that God is working in our lives when we stay the course and follow in obedience. If we are focused on someone else's road trip, wanting what they have, we are not making ourselves available for God to use us in a unique way based on our unique God-given talents that He bestowed upon us before birth. Oh, how grand an opportunity we have to make Jesus famous when we use our present journey to refine and hone in on our talents, to actually put them to kingdom use.

I look to a few of my friends as examples to keep me motivated to embrace my present road trip and allow God to shine His light on my talents and gifts. As I seek Him, I find passion in life by living in His purpose and call on my life versus my own agenda.

My friend Kelly is a graphic designer. Though she doesn't make Christian-focused material, her fresh perspective on life and God-given eye for the colorful, unique, and even edgy makes her an asset to her clients.

My friend Tori, a former saleswoman, might sometimes wish she were still living the fast-paced life of travel and company perks on days when her toddler's whining grates on her nerves. But she is grateful for this present season in life and makes her home beautiful for her family, as she now has time to cultivate her passion for decorating, sewing, and painting. Her family thrives in this nurturing and encouraging environment that she and her husband have established.

My friend Julie is an executive at a large nonprofit organization, with new responsibilities placed on her plate daily. She is often stretched to her limit but recognizes this opportunity to utilize her God-given skills for leadership. She exemplifies the humility in leadership that the Bible commands us to display. Her staff looks up to her and appreciates how much she cares about them as people and the success of the organization as a whole.

My mom, Iris, a newly retired teacher, embraced many classes full of challenging preschoolers over the years. We all know that teachers don't receive enough pay to compensate for the important work they do day in and day out. My mom didn't let the lack of pay keep her from affecting countless children's lives, as her hugs were always plentiful, her discipline always fair, her classroom always filled to the brim with decor to inspire growth and learning. Mom looked at her work as mission work. She loved those children, even during the most challenging days because Jesus loved them first.

Without prayer, the noise of the world drowns out the holy and pure in our lives and distracts us from our God-given direction.

All of this talk about road trips, journeys, and God's righteous and right ways might very well swirl around your brain and present a very important question: How do I know I'm even on that righteous or right path? To be honest, this is a question we should toss around and pray through on a regular basis—it keeps us on the road to spiritual maturity and prepares us to better embrace the turns and curves of this journey. I think you will be pleased to know that much of what we've already covered in our conversation about rising up will in fact, answer this question.

- If we are daily living in obedience to God's commands and feeding on His Word, our compass will point to true north as our life and heart condition pleases God. Though sin might distract us on our journey, we know from our discussion on bowing low that God is quick to forgive a repentant heart. Those lessons we learn from mistakes and sin only serve to enrich our journey.
- Staying in constant prayer throughout the journey refreshes our perspective as we recalibrate our hearts and minds to listen to God in still, quiet moments before Him at His throne. Though we may not hear audible words from God regarding our purpose or plan in life, it is through daily prayer that God gives us our daily bread (what we need for the day and what He wants us to do in worship of Him in that moment), and step-by-step He reveals how He is doing big things in our lives. Without prayer, the noise of the

world drowns out the holy and pure in our lives and distracts us from our God-given direction.

- Feelings of peace and contentment are key indicators that we are on God's righteous path for our lives. When we have to make a decision, if, after prayer and feeding on God's Word, there is a stirring in our heart—a sense of confusion or discontent—about the subject, that may be a clue that we need to take more time on the decision. A sense of peace about our present season in life or about an important decision is more than just a fleeting feeling. Peace is the Holy Spirit of God moving in your life to highlight the fact you are where God wants you to be.
- A life full of worship of the King and a grateful heart full of thanksgiving keep us focused on the One who is most important, even more important than the journey itself. On the good days and even the drama-filled days, by praising God for His goodness, for His strength, we find joy in the here and now rather than looking at what could be in the future or what should have been in the past.

This checklist of sorts is definitely not all-encompassing, but it does keep our eyes on the road ahead as we trust that God's ways are right and righteous. Some days our journey will seem daunting and frightening, especially when we don't see the clear path at the moment. Other days what God is asking us to do out of obedience puts us in a state of paralysis. Stalling out is often my particular method of dealing with feelings of doubt or fear. On days when I feel inadequate and intimidated, I would rather hide away, get my hands messy with craft paint, and lose myself in a painting instead of being brave and trusting that God knows what He is doing. Do you have one of those methods to hide away or shy away? Instead, let's be bold, let's be brave, and let's RISE UP! to push through fear as we cling to this exhortation in God's Word:

> You see, God did not give us a cowardly spirit but a powerful, loving, and disciplined spirit. (2 Tim. 1:7)

The unknown road ahead must not be forged with a spirit and attitude of cowardice or fear. The truth is, as much as we try to muster up our own version of bravery and boldness, we will fall short and burn out. But when we allow God to fill in the gap, when we open ourselves for His Spirit to pour out power, strength, and love, our righteous journey will be successful.

We will dig deeper into our new perspective of a fulfilled, successful life in the next section. In the meantime, will you take a moment to praise God that His ways are right and righteous? Can you wrap your mind around the idea that God allows us to join Him in His kingdom work and lays out a path for us to follow to do just that?

> *You leave us breathless* when Your awesome works answer us by putting everything right. (Ps. 65:5a)

Take some time to sift through this in the following Journal section.

Journal 3
THE RIGHTEOUS ROAD TRIP

- [ ] Let's do some "rubber meets the road" journaling in light of our road trip theme. Take a second to do a short little exercise to help solidify this in your heart. Copy 2 Timothy 1:7 in your journal. With your pen, draw a square around the word God. If a square is not your style, doodle whatever you have to in order to highlight God in this verse—arrows, stars, whatever!
- [ ] Now, instead of the word "us" write your name. Like this:

> You see, God did not give ____________ a cowardly spirit but a powerful, loving, and disciplined spirit.

- [ ] After reading my "vent" about flat and foundationless motivational phrases and thought-processes (such as "DREAM BIG!" or "IMAGINE!") do you see the importance of leaning on the power and strength (promised 2 Timothy 1:7), the love and direction that comes from God instead of a self-focused or lofty dream?
- [ ] We don't have to miss out on the excitement that we think comes from dreaming big when we seek God to do big things in our lives. How do you see the act of rising up lending itself to an exciting life journey?
- [ ] What are some times when you looked to someone else's life journey and wished you had the success, love life, family, money, or career, that that person has? What kind of feelings does this type of thinking drag up?
- [ ] How do you think trust and faith in God's perfect plan for your life (His righteous ways in Psalm 145:17) will spur you toward

living out your God-given talents? Do you get nervous or afraid of big requirements God might ask you to do in your life to make His name famous?

RISE UP! In Prayer

May I take a moment to pray for you as you contemplate the journey or road God has you on at this present time?

Father God, I thank You for my friend and what You are doing in her life as she chooses to RISE UP! and yield to Your righteous ways for her life. Help her to live obedient to Your call on her life and to see her main purpose is in seeking after You with a life full of worship. O God, when this righteous journey You have her on seems tough or daunting, help her to lean in close to You and not allow discouragement to derail her from rising up. Give her peace when the road ahead seems foggy. Let Your Word speak directly to her heart, and bestow on her Your wisdom. When she draws near to You, Lord, we will trust that You will draw near to her as your Word promises in James 4:8. In Jesus' name, amen!

God Does Big Things In Us

I'd like to check in with those reading this chapter who desperately want to RISE UP! and seek God but yet have no clue what the dreams and purposes even are that God may or may not have planted in their hearts. Hear me say this: if you have cultivated a desire to make Jesus famous, if you are living a life of praise with God's kingdom as your main perspective, you are right where you need to be. This is especially where our waiting in expectation comes in. For you, right now, the act of rising up may be to simply walk daily in trust and faith, knowing He has plans for you, to reveal in His perfect time, His perfect place, and His perfect manner.

There's a verse that I've read in passing before and probably even doodled on a note to a friend as a means of encouragement to her. God reminds us of His Word at just the right times for encouragement. I've got this heaviness on my heart in my own journey to RISE UP!, as I want to be used by God. He has planted dreams in my heart, but doors have yet to open to allow me to fully walk through and live these dreams out. I hide ideas and plans in my heart, often checking to make sure they came from the Lord and not from my own fancies. If you don't quite identify with this, know that it is okay. But if the idea of joining God in His kingdom work and making Him famous gets your heart pumping, that means the Lord is working in you and through you. Here's that verse:

> I am confident that the Creator, who has begun such a great work among you, will *not stop in mid-design but will* keep perfecting you until the day Jesus the Anointed, *our Liberating King, returns to redeem the world.* (Phil. 1:6)

This great work God is doing in our lives starts with the work God does inside our hearts and minds. The word work is appropriate in my opinion as I imagine Jesus using His gardening tools while digging up roots of pride and jealousy in my heart, patting down fresh soil of trust and peace, watering my God-given talents. And if we believe Scripture, He will continue to toil, root out, plant afresh, and grow beautiful blooms in my life and yours—blooms that will RISE UP! and flourish. Even a novice gardener like me knows that before a plant comes to full bloom time, care, pruning, watering, and sunlight are in order. This is the inner work God is doing in our lives and is right in line with personal evaluation of our sin, leading to repentant hearts, as we talked about in chapter 3.

What if this great work which God is doing in our generation and in each of our lives as individuals starts with a major work in the depths of our souls? What if instead of sending us out to do great things in His name, He first sent us inward to the places in our hearts that might prevent us from succeeding in the bold life choices that come with rising up? What if this movement of making Jesus famous is spurred on by actions such as personal

- revival?
- restoration?
- broken-down walls?
- dissolved fear?

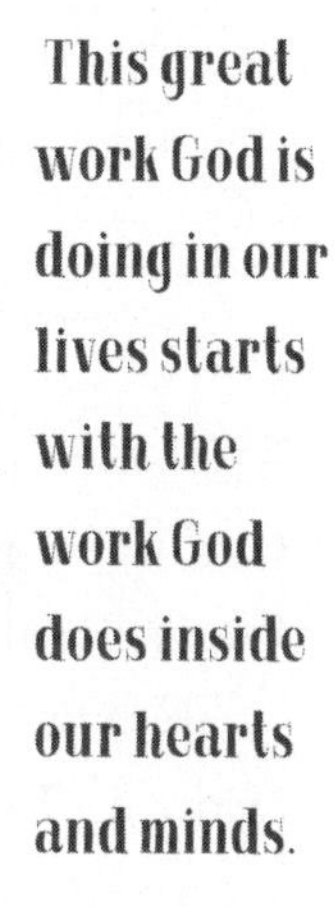

This great work God is doing in our lives starts with the work God does inside our hearts and minds.

How much more would the world recognize the great name of Jesus if we lived revived in the Holy Spirit and His power? How much more would we thrive in our God-given talents if we allowed Him to restore us back to the beauty He originally created in us before we had our own way in our lives? If walls lie unbroken around our hearts and we are unwilling to allow God to do His work to crush them, we won't be emotionally available to reach out to others in love.

You may remember my friend Chelsey, whom I mentioned in chapter 1, whose stress through nursing school led her to dwell on fear instead of focusing on God's goodness and faithfulness. A career in nursing was Chelsey's dream, one she hid in her heart and clung to with tight fists.

We are blocked from finding our purpose and passion in life when we place our own dreams on an ivory pedestal.

For His own divine reasons, God recently shut the door on her dream, and she was heartbroken. I was heartbroken for her! But what God has done in my friend's heart and life since He closed that door is so much more fruitful than any ideas of career advancement. Chelsey found herself with a choice: to seek after God and His presence or to allow what seemed like a setback in life to further her doubt and distrust in Jesus. Chelsey chose the former.

On her journey Chelsey chased after God instead of her need for a dream career or a purpose. In turn, God chased after her, pursued her, and restored her faith and trust in Him. Our God is relentless in His pursuit of our hearts. He restores us when we release our need for anything else (a dream included) over Him. We are blocked from finding our purpose and passion in life when we place our own dreams on an ivory pedestal. What God has for us in the restoration back to a satisfying relationship with Him will catapult us into a life where we can't help but make Him famous.

Just as we did in the previous section, where we asked the question "How do I know I'm on the righteous path?" I invite you to look introspectively at your present season in life and evaluate what God is doing in you—what He is teaching you, or growing and maturing in you. I have to warn you though, this introspection might be a bit painful. Lately God has been working on my full trust in Him as I'm forced to live in the today and not try to plan for the tomorrow. Those plans I've attempted to formulate for tomorrow are not panning out, and I can't explain why except it is simply God. We must not allow our present circumstances or even our dreams and plans to define who we are or what we believe about God. I encourage you to intentionally acknowledge the work that God is doing within you. I also encourage you to give that inner heart work more value and attention. We see in Scripture how God tips the scales on the value of what is going on in our hearts, the work He is doing in us.

> For the eyes of the LORD run to and fro throughout the whole earth, to show Himself strong on behalf of those whose heart is loyal to Him. (2 Chron. 16:9a NKJV)

I see this introspection as a means of preparation for what God will do in and then with our lives. This transformation in our hearts sets the foundation for God's plans and purpose to better take root as we flourish in His desires instead of our own. By not focusing on the dream or purpose itself but the steps along the journey, the growth and maturity, the restoration and revival, our rising up movement not only makes Jesus famous but conforms us to His image. We can't show the world the fame of Jesus if we are not emulating His character—His grace, His mercy, His forgiveness, His love. Whatever that dream and purpose planted in our hearts might be, however noble, the fact is that we were created to use that purpose for God's glory first and foremost. This starts with allowing God to do His great work in our hearts. By opening ourselves up to His handiwork within us, we make ourselves vulnerable, yes. But just as Psalm 145:17 says, our Lord is ever so kind and gracious in His ways. He holds our hearts with so much care and love. Sometimes the work in us is painful at the moment as He roots out junk in our hearts that keeps us blocked from fulfilling our God-given purpose.

Are you ready for God to do big things in your life?

So the question is, are you ready for God to do big things in your life? Do the words revival and restoration ring in your brain and get your heart pumping? That is the Holy Spirit beckoning you to say yes. The world around us needs to see bold, revived faith in those who claim to be Jesus' believers. They also need to see us restoring our relationship with the Lord, making Him the center of every square inch of our lives. Ask God for these big things, that

He will do His work, and trust what Scripture says for those who pray these bold prayers,

> The LORD is near to all who call upon Him, to all who call upon Him in truth. (Ps.145:18 NKJV)

Some translations of Psalm 145:18 state that the Lord is near to all who pray sincerely, with integrity. May our prayers for big things in our lives be lifted out of honest hope that from big things within us, God will use us in big ways for His kingdom. Let's pray with the bold realization that we need God to do His work in us because we are not equipped to RISE UP! in our own strength, as we cling to our own dreams and plans.

Now let's dig into a conversation about restoration and revival. Join me in the next section with your heart willing to explore your need and a pen ready to write it down in prayer!

Journal 4
GOD DOES BIG THINGS IN US

I often like to read the beginning passages of Genesis to remind myself of who God created me to be. He created a beautiful garden for man (and woman!) to have connection with Him in deep, meaningful relationship. Though Adam and Eve ate the forbidden fruit, disobeyed God, and created a chasm between creation and God's presence, God still cultivates this beautiful garden in our hearts and lives because of the work Jesus did on the cross.

In this section I mention the words restoration and revival as ways that God is working in us—doing big things in us. The Genesis account comes to mind again as we seek God's presence in our lives while we RISE UP! That very beauty which God created in the garden of Eden is represented in us when we live in restoration and revival and connect with the Maker of the universe.

☐ Take a few quiet moments to read through Genesis 1 and 2. Do you see the beauty and communion God created for Adam and Eve with Him? What does it mean to you personally that God restored this communion with you because of the sacrifice Jesus made on the cross?

Let's dig into the meaning of restoration and revival as we allow God to do big things in us.

> Restoration: The act of making something whole. Broken relationships, broken hearts, broken communion with God are made whole when we present them before the throne of the King. Jesus makes us whole again as we trust Him as our Savior, live our lives for Him, and devote ourselves to His kingdom.

Read Psalm 23:3 and take note of the phrase that reflects restoration in this verse:

> He makes me whole again, steering me *off worn, hard paths* to roads where *truth and* righteousness echo His name.

- ☐ Did you catch the word "again" in the first part of the verse? This reminds us that we are restored back to that complete communion and relationship with God that started in Genesis. What are your thoughts?
- ☐ What areas in your life need restoration? Do you need to restore any broken relationships with people in your life? Do you need to seek forgiveness and repentance (as we discussed in chapter 3)? How has any brokenness in your life kept you from rising up to make Jesus famous?

> Revival: An awakening. In some seasons of life we may feel blah and lack passion for God. In other seasons of life, we might live without the boldness to which God calls us for His Kingdom. Sometimes we need a daily revival and reminder that we have the very same power in us that raised Jesus from the dead three days after He died on the cross. This power conquers fears, breaks down walls, and extends grace. We are part of a generation of believers that are not living in this faith and power but instead with a bored, slumber-filled state of faith—just getting by everyday. We need revival! God deserves our revived faith and confidence in Him.
>
> Let us then fearlessly, confidently and boldly draw near to the throne of grace (the throne of God's unmerited favor to us sinners), that we may receive mercy [for our failures] and find grace to help in good time for every need [appropriate help and well-timed help, coming just when we need it]. (Heb. 4:16 AMP)

- [ ] What is your state of faith these days? Are you revived and ready to RISE UP? If not, what is going on in your life and in your heart where you need a revived faith and passion?
- [ ] How does Hebrews 4:16 stir your own personal revival?

RISE UP! In Prayer

Use the following prayer prompts to start a conversation with God about your own need for restoration and revival. Take some time in your own journal to write out your own prayers.

- Father, I need Your restoration in these areas of my life . . .
- I ask You to show me what full communion with You looks like because these areas in my life and heart are broken . . .
- Lord, I pray for a revived faith when I feel lack of passion . . .
- I pray that my generation of believers will RISE UP! in revived faith as You do big things in us and with us . . .

Do Life Differently: Rearranged Desires, Dreams, Purpose

I walked into my favorite arts and crafts store with a stack of gift cards burning a hole in my purse. Like a kid in a candy shop with an afternoon all to myself, I slowly walked aisle by aisle, captivated by all of the colors, textures, and possibilities. I normally walk into this place with some sort of a budget to keep a rein on my habit of going crazy buying colorful paper, neon paints, and the latest tools to make my art oh-so-much-better. (We tell ourselves that, right?) This day, I had no intention, no budget, a bunch of money, and the possibilities of all the crafty adventures I could take became paralyzing. Too many options. Too much stimulation. My mind reeled and my heart sank into a state of discouragement. I walked out overwhelmed. Not one bag in hand.

In a world full of choices, possibilities, and opportunities, do you ever feel overwhelmed? Recently several people in my life have shared with me their struggle with the question, what do I do with my life? This question is so similar to those we've chatted about together in this chapter. We are looking to seek after God and open our hearts for Him to plant desires, dreams, and purpose in our lives. The question—what do I do with my life?—has come, not just from friends who've recently graduated from school, but from a mom with school-age kids and more free time on her hands. My own mom is well into her sixties, just retired from a successful career as a teacher. The common theme I'm seeing here is the fact that all throughout our lives we are given opportunities to reevaluate what we are doing. Through changes in jobs, changes in family dynamics, new decades in life, this opportunity for evaluating our purpose and desires brings about opportunities to seek God and His presence, and even rearrange our desires and dreams so that we will align with His kingdom and make a difference with our lives.

Just as a candy shop promises that its endless array of sweets will satisfy us, the world around us tells us that success will satisfy us, so we search out careers to fulfill that itch to make a difference with our lives. We are often told that perfection, the perfect body, the perfect house (or apartment), the perfect wardrobe, or the perfect family gives us status and station in life. Oh, and let's not forget about another "candy shop" philosophy: that love and marriage will meet every need of our hearts. We have so many options around us, choices to make, that pull us every which way and confuse and discourage our hearts. We feel as if we will never measure up, never keep up, never be successful in life.

Let's look at how to stave off this overwhelming candy shop mentality and drill down to two passages in Scripture that help us to make sense of life around us. We'll start with Romans 12:1–2:

> Brothers and sisters, in light of *all I have shared with you about God's mercies,* I urge you to offer your bodies as a living and holy sacrifice *to God,* a sacred offering that brings Him pleasure; this is your reasonable, essential worship. Do not allow this world to mold you in its own image. Instead, be transformed *from the inside out* by renewing your mind. As a result, you will be able to discern what God wills and whatever God finds good, pleasing, and complete.

Be transformed from the inside out by renewing your mind.

This passage is pretty hardcore when we look at the first part, regarding our bodies (our lives) as a holy sacrifice to God. Let's not panic here, though. Throughout our conversation we have in essence covered this concept. In the Old Testament days, the Jews were required by God to regularly offer up various sacrifices in worship, in confession, and in repentance to the Lord. By killing animals or bringing the very best from their crops, they were making themselves right before God. But for us, as Jesus followers who believe that He died on the cross to be that sacrifice for us, we now have a new opportunity each day to offer our lives to God. Every time we choose to praise Him on good and bad days, every time we

This renewed mind and kingdom perspective will have us looking at life differently than before.

confess our sins, every time we choose His kingdom over our candy-shop world, we are offering ourselves as a holy sacrifice to God, and He finds it beautiful and pleasing.

But day in and day out, the tempting options in the world around us, the endless possibilities for success and "fulfillment" will try to lure us away from our journey to RISE UP! We must constantly conform to God's ways versus the ways of the world. God gives us a promise in Romans 12:2 that when we cling to Jesus, seek after Him above all else, and stay in His Word, He will give us the means to look at our lives and know what is meaningful (or "good"). We will have the eyes to see what will meet our desires and what dreams to follow when we have His truth hidden in our heart.

This renewed mind and kingdom perspective will have us looking at life differently than before. It will have us rearranging our desires.

A renewed mind, rearranged desires, transformed dreams . . . a woman who has these will

- love others more than herself and serve out of that love, allowing God to fulfill the deepest needs of her heart rather than expecting others to do so.
- live gratefully in the home God has blessed her with, using it as a place for hospitality and for welcoming others into a Holy Spirit–filled setting—regardless of her insecurities about the decor (or lack thereof).
- recognize the truth that raising godly children is of much more kingdom value than "keeping up with the Joneses" and overscheduling her family with activities.

- live responsibly with the resources God has given her, knowing that the thrill of retail therapy on a bad day doesn't last long.
- seek after a career as a means to make Jesus famous even at the workplace, instead of making plans simply out of drive for success.

A transformed dream, where career is concerned, might be a job where we use our God-given talents to make money so we can give more money away for God's kingdom work. Or it may be for those around us to see Jesus in us because we daily work with integrity to our best abilities.

With a renewed and transformed perspective (Rom. 12:1–2), let's rest in one more important truth:

> All *of you* who revere Him—God will satisfy your desires. (Ps. 145:19)

With all of our talk about dreams, desires, and purpose, I hope we don't lose sight of the fact that our Lord desires for us to enjoy the life He blesses us with. Some may see our discussion of God's plans and purpose for our life as a negation of living a life filled with excitement and thrills. This is so very far from the truth. God promises in His Word that Jesus came to give not just life but an overflowing and abundant life (John 10:10). There is ministry to do with our lives when we RISE UP!, yes, but there is also life to enjoy and thrive in.

"The thief approaches *with malicious intent*, looking to steal, slaughter, and destroy; I came to give life with joy and abundance." (John 10:10)

What changes for us with our new perspective is that we recognize that God alone fulfills our desires and purpose. Seeking Him first brings us to a new depth of seeing the world around us. We learn to distinguish what is fleeting and temporary about life and live for that which is eternal and satisfying to our hearts. The One who knows every hair on our heads, who hand crafted us for a specific purpose, knows what will make our hearts sing with delight. There is no need to chase tirelessly after dreams and purpose when we know we can rest in His presence to find true fulfillment of our desires. Rest in assurance that the desires God plants in our hearts and nurtures with His presence and His Word will not only bring us to wholeness but will also give us purpose.

Journal 5
DO LIFE DIFFERENTLY: REARRANGE YOUR DESIRES, DREAMS, PURPOSE

While I was writing this chapter, the Lord did a number on me and my heart. I am a dreamer. I like to contemplate and chew on and think about new and exciting goals. But I've learned to constantly evaluate those ideas I'm chewing on and present them before the Lord to see if they are from me or from His ultimate, best-laid plan.

Take some time in prayerful reflection over what God has said to you during this conversation about dreams, plans, and purpose.

Read through the following passages in Psalms and take some reflective time to write them in your own words based on our conversation in this chapter. We have already discussed two of the verses, so they should already be familiar.

> All *of you* who revere Him—God will satisfy your desires. (Ps. 145:19)

- [ ] Write this verse in your own words.

Now read the following verses:

> Trust in the LORD, and do good; Dwell in the land, and feed on His faithfulness. Delight yourself also in the LORD, And He shall give you the desires of your heart. (Ps. 37:3–4 NKJV)

> You have given him all he could wish for. After hearing his prayer, You withheld nothing. (Ps. 21:2)

- [ ] How will you do life differently as you seek Jesus and His presence in your life? How does this change your views on dreams and purpose? Take some time to write anything that comes to mind.

Notes

CHAPTER FIVE

RISE UP! WITH Influence

As we come to the final chapter, I'm tempted to tie a nice, pretty, tidy bow around this conversation and send you on your way to RISE UP! and make Jesus famous. But here's the deal: rising up and living out our faith is not always pretty and tidy. It is sometimes messy. When we choose to follow Jesus completely, He often puts us in places where we must get dirty. We have to get out of our comfort zones as we make time to love and serve others in what we will call our "sphere of influence." We've already talked about how we might do life and ministry with those around us, but let's actually look closer at who it is around us that needs to see Jesus. Who is floundering in life's drama and needs a hug and some truth as encouragement? Who is it that says she is a believer but yet lives in chains of doubt? Who in your life goes to church on Sundays just to check the box? Who is just doing life and missing out on the abundance that Jesus promises when we live in relationship with Him?

Are we willing to get messy?

Jesus did when He stepped off His heavenly throne to be human, to live life as we do, to feel our pain, to walk in our shoes . . . mess and all. You may be the only Jesus someone sees. You might be the only one who points someone to the hope and peace that God lavishes upon us. When we make ourselves available for God to use, He fills us with everything we need to get messy and make His name famous to those who are desperate for Him. We are all desperate for God, though many people in our lives need to be pointed to His loving arms. Many need to see how we live in relationship with the King of kings as we go about our day in even the mundane activities of life.

In our digital generation we find ourselves head down, thumbs pecking at the smartphone, with our minds distracted. Sometimes it is less messy to text than to look at a friend, recognize the pain in her eyes, and reach out to her by sharing her burden. It is easier to walk through the office and say, "Hi. How are you?" than to really probe and ask what's going on in a coworker's world. But Jesus requires more from us. He asks us to live out our faith, looking up beyond our selfish needs and see people through His eyes.

As I looked up the definition of influence, I noticed that the word is used both as a noun and as a verb. What caught my attention was more than the definition, such as making "impact" or having "effect." I was more concerned with the idea of influence being a verb, being an action. Too many Christians these days are stuck on the couch of complacency and are not rising up to influence (impact) their world because they just don't see the urgency in making Jesus famous.

So for us, simply put (yet not really that simple), influence equals pointing people to Jesus. It means reflecting who He is to anyone with whom we come in contact.

It is time for us to be brave and bold. It is also time for us to couple our bravery and boldness with love and kindness and mercy. Our brave actions will mean nothing if we do not love. Our bold lifestyle of rising up is worthless if we do not extend kindness right alongside it. We need to balance both sides of the coin, just as Jesus did. The bold sermons He preached were, some would say, brazen and outlandish for that day. But, what also drew people to the Lord was His never-failing love even for "the least of these" (see Matthew 25:31–46). The combination of brave/bold and love/mercy can only come from the Holy Spirit. For in our selfish natures, we can easily shy away from either side of the coin.

I want to introduce you to Brett, a writing buddy of mine. She is the real deal and is not afraid to make Jesus famous in her own sphere of influence. Join Brett and me as I pick her brain about rising up with influence.

SARAH Brett, what are your thoughts on the concept of rising up and making Jesus famous?

BRETT This is such a beautiful, special calling. And it's in every one of us. Once you realize that your life is built on nothing more than to make Christ known, everything else—careers, promotions, romance, families, even friendships—seems to grow strangely dim. Compared to the richness of a life lived in pursuit of Christ, nothing else ever really seems to satisfy.

SARAH I love how you said that the call to make Jesus famous is in every one of us. It's exciting to think about our opportunity to join in the work of God's kingdom at the very place God has us right here and right now. We all have a "sphere of influence," that is, we have people in our lives that we love, do life, work, and even work out with. When we choose to RISE UP!, we then have the daily privilege to be Jesus to the people in our sphere of influence. How do you define your sphere of influence?

BRETT I like to think of sphere of influence as an epicenter of an earthquake. Wherever you are planted, you drum and shake the world around you. The people with whom you work, your families, the roommates with whom you live, even baristas at your local coffee shop are affected by your joy (or crankiness) whether you realize it or not. We live in a relational world, and it's fun to think about how everyone you meet or make eye contact with are people you have the potential to reach in the name of Christ.

Brett is absolutely right. This call to make Jesus famous is for both introverts and extroverts. God gives each of us special character traits and talents that we can use to relate to those in our sphere of influence in the name of Jesus.

I asked Brett about any Bible figures that she looks to for inspiration to RISE UP! with influence. Brett described Esther as a woman who, "emulates the greatest aspect of what Christlike leadership and influence looks like." We chatted about how Esther operated under an, "If not me, then who?" attitude when she saw a need in her kingdom and filled it with dignity and servanthood.

I asked Brett what she thinks keeps women from rising up and influencing those around them to make Jesus famous. We agreed on two words: fear and insecurity. Brett brought up such a great point regarding the world's view of success and purpose. "These pursuits, these false ambitions, are deceptive. They're stationary bikes. You can pedal hard and fast, but you won't go anywhere. You will not be fulfilled."

Fear and insecurity come into play when we put too much stock in the opinions of others. Also, we may fear that we will not measure up, that we will mess up and embarrass Jesus if we RISE UP! in His name and make royal mistakes in our lives. But through our vulnerability, our willingness to share our sin and mess-ups, others will see God's forgiveness in action. They will want that forgiveness for themselves.

What the world around us needs, and what our personal sphere of influence needs, is not another "religious girl" to self-righteously slam the Bible in people's faces. No, the world needs to see us reflecting Jesus and living out His Word and promises even when life gets seriously messy.

Let's continue this conversation in the journal section to hone in on each of our personal spheres of influence. Grab your journal and pen.

- [ ] Take some time to evaluate who is in your sphere of influence. Here are some categories of life interactions to get you started. Keep in mind that your sphere of influence encompasses anyone with whom you have regular contact. Write down a few names that come to mind in each of the following categories:
    - Work
    - Gym
    - Friends (social groups)
    - Charity/service groups
    - People at your kids' school
    - Neighbors
    - Hobbies (running groups, people at the dog park, etc.)
    - Church
    - Regulars at your coffee shop (or whatever is your regular "place")

- [ ] The idea of your sphere of influence may start out as a bit overwhelming. Take some time right now to write out a prayer asking God to highlight just one person or area in your sphere that He wants you to interact with in a more meaningful way to make His name famous. If you already have a person or area of your sphere in mind, go ahead and start praying specifically!

- [ ] While we are in a place of openness to impacting our sphere of influence and making Jesus famous, let's recognize that for us to pour out our faith, we must continually come to the throne of our King and fill up on His wisdom, guidance, and truth. Let's find some encouragement in Colossians 2:6–7:

> Now that you have welcomed the Anointed One, Jesus the Lord, into your lives, continue to journey with Him *and allow Him to shape your lives*. Let your roots grow down deeply in Him, and let Him build you up on a firm foundation. Be strong in the faith, just as you were taught, and always spill over with thankfulness.

☐ In your journey to RISE UP! how do you allow God to "shape your life" these days? What benefit do you see in letting your "roots grow down deeply" in Jesus?

☐ How then, do these deep roots affect how you live your life day in and day out within your sphere of influence?

☐ Do you recognize how much more impact you have in your world when you are rooted in the Lord rather than cruising in life on your own path with your own agenda?

RISE UP! in Prayer

Use the following prayer prompts to guide you in conversation with the Lord.

- Lord, help me keep my eyes open as I go about my day to recognize who is in my sphere of influence and to whom it is that You want me to reach out . . .
- I pray that You will strengthen my faith as I dig my roots deep in You . . .

Influence on the Narrow Road

I have a weird obsession with reading spy thriller novels. I devour them. You know, the kind where super-secret good guys get the really, really bad guys? I like it even more when the spy is a woman who kicks butt. I know. I'm weird. I've been trying to figure out what exactly attracts me to these books and even movies. Yes, I'm the wife who begs her husband to take her on a date night to see the latest good-guy-gets-the-bad-guy movie. No chick flicks for me! Maybe it is the adrenaline rush that comes with reading fast-paced books. Maybe it is my love for the mysterious as I get a tiny peek into the life of a spy.

So when my friend introduced me to the latest spy cable TV show, I was all over it. I downloaded the first season and set it up in my workout room to give me some extra motivation to feel the burn. The first day I was taken aback a bit by the language and the very explicit sex scenes, but I kept watching. Even though I felt rather filthy after watching while working out (no, it was more than the sweat from squats and jumping jacks), after the first day I convinced myself it would be okay if I just fast-forwarded through the sex because the rest of the plot captivated me. A few days later, I felt a pit in my stomach, and I knew the Holy Spirit was speaking to me. Allowing my eyes to view filth and ears to hear such outright ugliness would infect the rest of my heart and mind eventually. Remember my old foul language habit? (See chapter 1.) The Bible clearly tells us to guard our hearts and minds for a reason. So, I obeyed and stopped watching. It was hard, if I'm honest. I did this because I recognized that I worship Jesus with my obedience to Him, and I know that He blesses obedience.

> **Authentic faith starts with steps of obedience to our Lord that we take even in secret.**

I use this seemingly small example of obedience to God because it is in even the small decisions that we are making Jesus famous in our hearts and lives. Authentic faith starts with steps of obedience to our Lord that we take even in secret, obedience only seen by God. These small steps of obedience and worship add up to large measures of deeply rooted faith and obedience that impact people around us. Have you noticed how people respond to authenticity? It makes them curious. When we walk through what Jesus calls the "narrow door," we influence people to take a peek in that door and possibly join us on the narrow road.

> *There are two paths before you; you may take only one path.* One doorway is narrow. *And one door is wide.* Go through the narrow door. For the wide door leads to a wide path, and the wide path is broad; the wide, broad path is easy, and the wide, broad, easy path has many, many people on it; but the wide, broad, easy, crowded path leads to death. Now then that narrow door leads to a narrow road that in turn leads to life. It is hard to find that road. Not many people manage it. (Matt. 7:13–14)

The choices we make toward obedience and thus, authentic faith, lead us down the Lord's "narrow road," which in its ultimate fulfillment is eternal life with Jesus in His kingdom. In its simplest definition, (yet, again, not that simple) the narrow doorway means that we choose Jesus as our Lord and one and only Savior. We choose to walk through that narrow doorway because we believe deep down to our core that He is God and no one and no other thing in this world is worthy of our devotion, faith, praise, and obedience. Oh, the wide door might seem tempting. There are many other options of whom or what we place our devotion and faith in this world. But once we make our choice, there is an even narrower road to walk before us. Don't mistake this narrow road as lacking excitement or fun or good times. For this road is rich with God's goodness along the way to heaven.

It is not always easy to choose the better way over that which tantalizes our eyes, attracts our attention, or piques our curiosity on the worldly wide road. That is why the Bible says that not many people will choose the narrow road. Dare I even say that those who claim they are religious will not daily choose the narrow road? May our authentic faith and thriving relationship with the Lord drive us daily to choose Him and bring those in our sphere of influence with us. Yes, it is hard. It is tough to put our carnal needs aside and allow Jesus to meet those needs with His ever-satisfying, ever-sustaining presence. Lest we grow tired and weary of doing the "right" thing, God promises that He is there. If we experience rejection because others don't understand this narrow road, He comforts and revives our passion. If we fear failure, fear of letting Jesus down with our choices, fear that others will reject this narrow road because of us, God extends a long arm of grace and forgiveness. Psalm 145 reminds us:

> All *of you* who revere Him—God will satisfy your desires. He hears the cries *for help,* and He brings salvation. (Ps.145:19)

God hears us when we cry out that the narrow road is too hard, and He saves us.

God hears us when we cry out that the narrow road is too hard, and He saves us. He hears us in our pleas for help when discouragement covers us and we feel that our authenticity in faith is not making an impact in our sphere of influence. It is God Himself who brings salvation. God brings His people to Him. We cannot save people, but we can allow God to work in us and shine the light on that narrow path.

So how are we relating to our sphere of influence as we walk down our narrow road? Does our authenticity come through as we talk about that special blessing God graced us with this very morning? Do we also express our royal mess-ups and how good God is in His lavish forgiveness? As we do life with people, we influence them to join us in rising up, to make their own decision to choose the narrow door instead of the one that the Bible says leads to destruction. Let's get real though. That destruction in its ultimate realization is hell. Some theologians say that the pain and destruction in hell comes from the lack of God's presence. Along the road, the wide road that leads to destruction and death, there is also a lack of God's abundant life and presence. It is our role to live in God's presence, giving people the opportunity to taste and see that God is good (Ps. 34:8). May we stand alongside our friends, our family, our coworkers, our fellow gym rats, and shine God's light through the narrow door, down the narrow road, and toward His satisfying presence.

Along the way of walking the narrow path, our own feet will get dirty.

This biblical concept of the narrow door and the proceeding narrow path we walk on in faith is a culmination of our entire conversation of rising up. Our kingdom perspective and desire for the eternal keeps our feet walking straight on this godly path. It also takes a large measure of humility and bowing low to Jesus alone as the wide path tempts us with other "little g" gods to give our time and passions. And let us remember that along this narrow path, we see God at work in us as we choose daily to do life differently.

It is interesting to imagine the dirt paths (narrow paths) upon which Jesus and His disciples walked in their day as they were spreading the gospel. With their sandals on, feet caked with sand and dirt, whenever they stopped in a house for food or rest, washing their feet was imperative. It was Jewish custom that a servant of the house wash a guest's feet, a sign of hospitality from the host.

During the Last Supper, Jesus kneeled and washed His disciples' feet as a pure and holy example of humility. Can you imagine? Our King of kings, who stepped down from His majestic throne to walk the earth with us, for us, actually kneeled and did the work of a servant. Along the way of walking the narrow path, our own feet will get dirty. We will get messy ourselves if we see the kingdom work before us as we serve others and love our enemies. Just as Jesus did, though, will we put our own needs and comfort aside to kneel with a water basin and towel in hand to "wash the feet" of others in our sphere of influence? Will we:

- wash their feet when we hand money to the homeless person on the corner of our regular coffee house and explain we are doing this in Jesus' name?
- wash their feet when we offer to babysit for a single mother who needs a break and when we pray with her?
- wash their feet by befriending the standoffish girl at work and let her see how Jesus gladdens your heart?
- wash their feet by collecting items needed for a local group going on an overseas mission trip?

Along the narrow path we keep our eyes open to the needs of others while we keep in mind that their ultimate need is fulfilled through the Lord. We can only be effective on this narrow path when we RISE UP! and make Jesus famous in our own life first and then proclaim His goodness and live it out before those we influence in life.

Journal 2
INFLUENCE ON THE NARROW ROAD

Living out our faith on the narrow road is all about doing life differently from what we've personally done in the past and absolutely differently from the world around us. We've talked already about doing life differently throughout our conversation. The image of the narrow road and the narrow door that precedes it brings us full circle to our daily decision of choosing to make Jesus famous in even the areas of our life that seem too tempting to pass up.

- ☐ Take a look back at my spy thriller TV show as an example of exactly this: choosing the narrow road by surrendering something we hold so dear in order to make Jesus famous. Sometimes choosing the narrow road is simply resisting temptation in Jesus' name! It is a place where we choose what is better, what is in line with God's Word, what we know pleases God. Make a list of "small temptations" that you see as choices between the narrow road and that tempting wide road.
- ☐ Now make a list of bigger choices in life where you choose the narrow road versus the wide, earthly road.
- ☐ Why do you suppose resisting even these seemingly small incidences of temptation add up to a big movement in our faith?
- ☐ We talked about how our faith becomes authentic as we choose the narrow versus the wide road and how that authenticity attracts people. A big chunk of our authenticity comes with obedience to God along that narrow road. What is our motivation for this obedience? Do we love Him and desire to worship Him with our obedience?

- [ ] In your Bible read and write out the following verses in your journal:
    - John 14:15
    - Why is love equated with obeying God's Word?
    - Luke 11:28

- [ ] What blessings do you see that come from obedience to God? (Example: Look at Galatians 5 for the fruit of the Spirit.)
- [ ] How does living out an authentic faith on the narrow road bless others as they see our real-life examples of making Jesus famous?

RISE UP! in prayer . . .

Join me in prayer journaling Psalm 145:19. Use the following prompts to get you started.

> All of *you who* revere Him—God will satisfy your desires. He hears the cries *for help,* and He brings salvation.

- Lord, Jesus! I praise Your name in reverence and fear. You are almighty, worthy . . .
- I hand over my heart to You in trust that You will rearrange my desires and align them with Your glory and kingdom plan . . .
- Lord, it is hard choosing the narrow road, but I know I will find life and fulfillment on that road. I trust that You hear my cry for help as I take steps down Your narrow road . . .
- Help me build my trust in You and Your provision and strength, God, as I cry out for You daily. I trust that You will save me, You will reach Your strong arm down, pick me up, and help me back on the narrow road when I walk astray . . .

Compelled to Follow the Leader

Do you remember the kid in grade school who, at the end of the day, when you all thought your teacher forgot to assign homework, raised her hand to remind said teacher? Yep. That was me. In my mind I didn't want to return to school the next day with the teacher expecting our homework finished, but alas we didn't have it to work on to begin with. Goody Two-shoes, that's what I am. I am a rule-follower who secretly, very secretly, is intrigued by those who walk to their own drumbeat and even bend the rules . . . sometimes.

When I reread a very familiar passage about Jesus calling His first disciples, something new piqued my interest.

> *One day* Jesus was walking along the Sea of Galilee when He saw Simon (also called Peter) and Andrew throwing their nets into the water. They were, of course, fishermen.
>
> **Jesus:** *Come,* follow Me, and I will make you fishers of men.
>
> Immediately Peter and Andrew left their fishnets and followed Jesus.
>
> Going on from there, Jesus saw two more brothers, James the son of Zebedee and his brother John. *They, too, were fishermen.* They were in a boat with their father Zebedee getting their nets ready to fish. Jesus summoned them, *just as He had called to Peter and Andrew,* and immediately they left their boat and their father to follow Jesus. (Matt. 4:18–22)

Let's take a moment to put ourselves in these men's shoes, or sandals. After hearing Jesus' voice, His call on their life to join Him in ministry, they followed the Lord immediately. Right away these men put down their nets, put down their familiar way of life, put down and set aside status quo to follow Him. It even says that the brothers James and John left their father to follow this intriguing man who called their names. This was, in fact, against all custom, for young men were expected to follow Jewish tradition and stay in the same line of work as their fathers.

As a chronic rule-follower, I can't get over that these men immediately upheaved their lives, went against the cultural norm, and followed Jesus. No questions asked. But, we might be inclined to ask these questions . . .

- What was it about Jesus that compelled them toward such a drastic and bold lifestyle change?

  Compel is a word that I chose to use in this question because for me, it describes this drawing-in quality that characterizes our Lord. Our Lord draws us in with His compassionate yet authoritative nature. We step closer to Jesus because He draws out of us a love for Him that was born in us from our creation. Have you ever taken a moment to imagine the look of love in His eyes as He gazes upon each of us? Whether people love, serve, and worship Jesus or despise and use His name in vain, no one can deny that Jesus compels notice. Will we choose to move forward and follow Jesus or counter that compelling nature by stepping back from His call?

- What did Jesus see in these fishermen that equipped them to live as devoted disciples and even revolutionaries?

  We cannot presume to know what exactly Jesus saw deep in their hearts. As we've discussed already, we know that God plants His purpose, talents and dreams in our hearts if we align ourselves with His desires versus our own agenda. Maybe Jesus saw in their souls a hunger for God. Maybe He saw an openness in their hearts to put aside their own comforts to walk that narrow road toward God's glory. An open and humble heart, a soul hungry for Him, a willingness to obey His Word, and a readiness to make Jesus our priority is all the qualification we need to be called by Him and make a difference with our lives. Jesus fills in the gaps where we are inadequate.

- Do we shy away from our call to follow because insecurity, fear, or doubt keeps us from setting aside our "fishing nets" to heed His voice?

I wonder if the thought that you are not qualified to be used by God keeps you from rising up and making Jesus famous. Be encouraged in the fact that the disciples Jesus called were regular men, not well-educated rabbis of their time, and were neither rich nor influential. What did qualify them to heed the call of Jesus was their willingness to follow, no matter what they would be asked to give up along the way.

This now begs the question, how can we authentically live out our faith and impact others if we do not loosen our tight grip on our personal "nets" and lay them down?

Our nets might carry those "little g" idols we've previously discussed, anything we put as priority on a pedestal above God. For me lately, the net that God is calling me to put down to follow Him consists of relinquishing control of my life, my family, my job (everything I hold very near and dear to my heart), and taking steps down that narrow road in pure, sometimes blind faith. Sometimes our nets hold our fear of failure. Sometimes they hold a need for others' approval. What if we let God down and fail because we've sinned (which is inevitable)? What will others think of our decision to live differently and make Jesus famous?

I give all of these examples because the contents of our nets will change and evolve as we journey down the narrow road. What we hold so tightly one day will be relinquished over to the Lord as He does big things in us. Then, the next day, it is another net full to hand over. We must make a daily choice to lay down what we hold tight, what we prioritize, what we hold dear, to follow Jesus. With that daily decision comes a faith ever stronger, ever bolder, ever glorifying to God day in and day out.

Journal 3
COMPELLED TO FOLLOW THE LEADER

- [ ] As we are winding down our conversation within these pages (hopefully it will be an ongoing conversation between you and Jesus), I'm wondering how your view of rising up has changed from page 1 to now. Specifically, how has your view of following Jesus transformed? Are you even more willing to lay down your net?
- [ ] What are you still reluctant to let go of? What is keeping you from moving forward to follow Jesus with abandon?

I ask these questions for us to continually use to evaluate in our lives. Once I think I've made the good, Jesus-girl decision and laid down a net that is near and dear to me, the Holy Spirit shows me yet another net. Let's find joy in our constant movement toward a mature faith rather than frustration that there are more nets to lay down.

> Don't run from tests and hardships, brothers and sisters. *As difficult as they are, you will ultimately* find joy in them; if you embrace them, your faith will blossom under pressure *and teach you true patience* as you endure. *And true patience brought on by* endurance will equip you to complete the long journey *and cross the finish line*—mature, complete, and wanting nothing. (James 1:2–4)

- [ ] In your own words, paraphrase the above scripture.
- [ ] What would you say to the notion that our movement of rising up to make Jesus famous and laying down our nets is one we work on—by the power of the Holy Spirit—on a daily basis? Does it encourage you or discourage you, based on this scripture? Why?

Some days we may very well be discouraged as we loosen our tight grip on our lives that we'd rather not hand over to Christ. It is tough to sacrifice, to put down, what is comfortable and familiar to follow Jesus down that often unfamiliar narrow path. But let's find strength in the fact that we follow the King of kings. Jesus made the ultimate sacrifice on the cross. He shed blood for us, for our sins, so that we can—by His power—have strength to lay down our nets to follow Him.

☐ In your mind, how does the concept of laying down what we hold in high priority to follow Jesus apply to the topic of influencing others to make Jesus famous in their lives? What kind of example do we set for our sphere of influence when we, ourselves, are compelled to lay down our nets and follow Him?

RISE UP! in Prayer

Use the following prayer prompts to guide you in conversation with the Lord. Write out your prayers in your journal.

- Father God, give me the desire to daily lay down my net and follow You, especially in these areas of my life . . .
- Lord, I thank You for blessing me with joy and patience and so much more when I follow You, and as my faith matures . . .

Full Circle

Circles. Circles are all around us. They are probably something we see with our eyes, but because they are everywhere, we don't always recognize them. We find circles in philosophy: the circle of life. We find circles in art via patterns and repetition. We find circles in astronomy because yeah . . . the earth is round, not flat. We find circles in mechanics and engineering in the simplest form of the wheel. We also find circles in toys, like the yo-yo and the hula hoop. If you took a look at my personal journal, you would find tons of oddly shaped circles, as it is my go-to doodle pattern. And, based on my quick study of circles on the World Wide Web, apparently there is no man-made perfect circle. Well, that's a relief!

The phrase "coming full circle" is one that conjures up a feeling of completion for me. This is an elusive feeling, as I quite often neglect to complete tasks throughout my day. Do you? Sometimes my brain is moving in so many different directions that I'm on to the next thought or the next project before I've finished the first one. Prime examples: walking out of the house for the day after applying eyeliner on only one eye or shaving only one leg in the shower. And I'd rather not mention the pile of clothing in my closet, lying there in wrinkles awaiting a hanger.

It is up to us to constantly circle back to His presence throughout our day-to-day drama and benefit from this satisfying feeling of completion.

The idea of completion or "full circle" might nurture our restless or scattered minds and souls when we soak in this not-so-elusive truth. Making Jesus the center of our lives results in the recognition that God has His bigger plan; God has His bigger plan—and part of His ultimate kingdom agenda is already complete. As Jesus took His final breath on the cross, He said, "It is finished." Three days later, He rose from the dead, victorious over sin and death—for each and every one of us. It is up to us to constantly circle back to His presence throughout our day-to-day drama and benefit from this satisfying feeling of completion. It is also up to us not to worry whether we are making a difference in our sphere of influence. God already has the end result planned as we love and serve those around us. That's all that we have to do: make Jesus famous, love Him first, and love others. He will take care of the rest.

The messiness I wrote about in the introduction to this chapter often comes from doing what God commands within our sphere of influence. (See, there's a circle again!) How often are we pouring out our time, our talents, and our energy, but not usually seeing the fruit of our labor? How often do we pray diligently that a friend will come to the Lord but never see answers to that prayer? It can be discouraging. This frustration comes from our results-based focus rather than a focus and trust in God's full-circle, bigger kingdom plan. In the meantime, we find ourselves in a place of depletion and exhaustion.

As you do life and ministry in your sphere of influence, find freedom in handing the results of your kingdom work over to the One who owns it all anyway. This is not to negate the impact we make because of Jesus working in and through our lives. Why don't we offer up empty hands in surrender? These empty hands, this giving up control, leads us to a crucial element of our mission to RISE UP!

Get Filled Up to RISE UP!

It may surprise you to know that rising up requires filling up before you can pour out God's love and fame on others. That's because our desire to impact our sphere of influence only goes so far. For we are human with human limits in our capacity to extend grace and mercy. Our passion to make Jesus famous only goes so far before pride creeps in and it becomes all about us rather than all about Him. I find it intriguing how the author of our Psalm 145, who sat on his own kingly throne as he led the nation of

Israel, constantly circled back to worship and proclaiming the fame of the Lord above his own kingly name. Let's examine the final verse in Psalm 145 as David finishes the psalm right where he started it: in all-out praise of the King.

> My lips will sing the praise of the Eternal. Let every creature *join me* and praise the holy name of God—forever and always! (Ps. 145:21)

To do this in our own lives, to constantly circle back to worship, we must fill up on the Holy Spirit daily—no, minute by minute, even. We must . . .

- refresh and fan the flame. Our passion for making Jesus famous should be much more than an emotional high. There will be days when we may not feel God's power and presence in our lives, but that doesn't mean they are not there. Just as David always circled back to worship in His psalms, we need to find our way back to the throne of the King, kneeling in humble worship even when we don't feel like it. That act of obedience refreshes our perspective on life and faith. Be refreshed with the knowledge that though you have an integral place in God's kingdom, He is bigger than any deficits in our own strength and humanness. He will fill in the gaps by leading us with His ultimate wisdom and truth. We don't have to forge our own way in the world around us.
- reset our focus. Even in our most fired-up moments and seasons in life, we are susceptible to that which steals our laser focus on Jesus. We may even get caught up in the religious aspect of making Jesus famous as we do many great acts in His name yet lose track of why we are doing those great things. The apostle Paul exhorted us to do just this: reset and refocus.

> *So it comes down to this:* since you have been raised with the Anointed One, *the Liberating King,* set your mind on heaven above. The Anointed is there, seated at God's right hand. Stay focused

> on what's above, not on earthly things, because your *old* life is dead and gone. Your *new* life is now hidden, enmeshed with the Anointed who is in God. On that day when the Anointed One—who is our very life—is revealed, you will be revealed with Him in glory! (Col. 3:1–4)

Setting our focus on what is above keeps us ultimately grounded in what is of utmost importance: worshipping and loving God with all of our hearts, souls, minds, and strength. (See Luke 10:27.)

- daily live re-captivated by God's glory. God's glory is not natural to this sin-filled, war-torn, hurting world we live in. It is supernatural. But it is also a natural human tendency to grow apathetic or make normal in our minds and hearts what is, in fact, supernatural. To battle apathy, an appetite for allowing God to re-captivate us daily is essential. Again David reminds us of the freedom that only comes from being captivated by God's glory.

> Your majesty and glorious splendor *have captivated me;* I will meditate on Your wonders, *sing songs of Your worth*. We confess—there is *nothing greater than You, God,* nothing mightier than Your awesome works. I will tell of Your greatness *as long as I have breath*. (Ps. 145:5–6)

Let our hearts explode with the wonder of God's goodness, apparent around us if we choose to acknowledge it. Let our mouths sing notes of praise to the one who is worthy. Let our actions tell of God's personal works in our lives that bring us to completion in Christ.

- revisit the cross. Yes the sacrifice Jesus made on the cross is once and for all. God broke the barrier between our sin-filled nature and His glory through the blood shed by our King Jesus, the perfect Lamb that was slain. His grace, that free gift of life bestowed upon us, never falls short. Where the deficit lies is often in our inability to internalize and live out this reality.

Daily we must nail to the cross—put to death—our pride. We must surrender our need for security in earthly matters. We must kneel at the cross and hand Him our agenda. The resurrection of our Lord, Jesus––that He rose from the grave in all power and authority––should motivate us to RISE UP! and lift up His name above our own so that the world, and especially those in our individual spheres, will see through us and see His greatness.

Full circle . . .

It all starts with Jesus.
It all ends with Jesus.
What will we do with the in-between?

Journal 4
FULL CIRCLE

As I continue to study Psalm 145, I keep finding new, intriguing nuggets in which to soak. We noted that the final verse of Psalm 145 circles back to where it started: in praise of the eternal King.

- ☐ What are your thoughts on our "coming full circle" concept and sense of completion that comes with it? How has God brought you full circle in your faith journey of rising up?

David, the author of our Psalm 145, invites us to join him in praising the Lord . . .

> My lips will sing the praise of the Eternal. Let every creature *join me and* praise the holy name of God—forever and always! (Ps. 145:21)

- ☐ What intrigues me about this invitation to join him in praising God is the idea that I, too, can invite those in my world to join in on the praise and worship. But the question is, how do we go about doing this? What is it about our life and faith that invites people to join in?

To be effective in our rising up, filling up on and soaking in God's presence is essential. How will you . . .

- ☐ refresh and fan the flame?
- ☐ reset your focus?
- ☐ be re-captivated?
- ☐ revisit the cross?

RISE UP! in Prayer

Use the following prayer prompts to guide you in conversation with the Lord.

- Lord, compel my soul to circle back to You when I feel . . .
- Help me, Jesus, to be bold and brave in my everyday faith while I invite others to join me in worship of You . . .

Conversation Conclusion

As a benediction of our conversation together, would you mind if I prayed for you again? This passage in Hebrews spoke volumes to me one day when I mulled through if or how or when I, personally, am rising up with integrity and purpose, truly for the fame of Jesus. What spurs me forward in the journey is the freedom that comes with giving God the glory in my life rather than striving to make my own name famous. What also makes me say, "Heck yeah!" is the freedom that comes from God doing His work through me versus me creating just nice, good things to do to live my life differently. I hope you will see what I mean when you read Hebrews 13:20–21.

> Now may the God of peace who brought up our Lord Jesus from the dead, that great Shepherd of the sheep, through the blood of the everlasting covenant, make you complete in every good work to do His will, working in you what is well pleasing in His sight, through Jesus Christ, to whom be glory forever and ever. Amen. (NKJV)

Lord, our King Jesus. We lift You up and praise Your holy name. I thank You for my friend who chose to RISE UP! and do life differently for Your fame alone. As she travels alongside You and chooses that narrow road, I know that You will be her God of peace. I pray that she will choose to sit at Your heavenly throne daily and dwell in your peace. For it is in that peace that she will do the work which You have called her to do. Great Shepherd, You are our leader, our protector and guide. I ask that You will cover my friend's heart when the weight of the world threatens to crush her will to continue to do the sometimes hard. Help her to see that You, her Shepherd, are worthy and that the trials of this present time will fade when she sees You face-to-face one day.

We proclaim over our lives that by the blood of the everlasting covenant, You, Jesus, made her righteous and holy in Your sight. It is all because of the cross. Help her, Lord, to see that she is clean and beautiful in Your loving eyes. Thank You for the cross, Jesus. I pray that each day she will turn to you to be equipped to do Your kingdom work. Help my friend to see that she simply must use what You give her here and now in life. Give her strength to refrain from wanting the gifts, talents and opportunities that you have given others. Her gifts come straight from You; help her to see how You tailor-made her for Your kingdom work. It is to You that we give glory forever and ever; not our fame, but Yours alone, King Jesus.
Amen!

I would like for the following prompts to serve as a way for us to recap our RISE UP! journey. The following pages are a place to refer back to when you need encouragement to keep doing life differently—to keep rising up. Prayerfully journal through what spoke to you most in each chapter. What challenged you? What scripture inspired you?

Let's not simply shut this book and move on with our lives. Let's do this together. Keep rising up, my friend, and make Jesus famous!

Take a while to rewrite Psalm 145 in its entirety as a way to seal in your heart and mind the motivation to just RISE UP!

Take a moment to flip back to each chapter and write your answers to the following prompts in your journal.

Chapter 1: A Life of Praise

- Scripture that stood out and challenged me. (Write the verse in your journal.)
- The main thing: One main idea in this chapter that encouraged me to RISE UP!
- What now? How will you do life differently regarding this main thing?

Chapter 2: Be Kingdom Minded

- Scripture that stood out and challenged me. (Write the verse in your journal.)
- The main thing: One main idea in this chapter that encouraged me to RISE UP!
- What now? How will you do life differently regarding this main thing?

Chapter 3: Bow Low Before You RISE UP!

- Scripture that stood out and challenged me. (Write the verse in your journal.)
- The main thing: One main idea in this chapter that encouraged me to RISE UP!
- What now? How will you do life differently regarding this main thing?

Chapter 4: Our Dreams, Purpose, and God's Agenda

- Scripture that stood out and challenged me. (Write the verse in your journal.)

- The main thing: One main idea in this chapter that encouraged me to RISE UP!
- What now? How will you do life differently regarding this main thing?

Chapter 5: RISE UP! with Influence

- Scripture that stood out and challenged me. (Write the verse in your journal.)
- The main thing: One main idea in this chapter that encouraged me to RISE UP!
- What now? How will you do life differently regarding this main thing?

Notes

Conversation Starter

Just Keep It Simple

Too many things in life are too complicated, and this includes women's Bible study groups. So, in an effort to encourage you to gather a group of friends to converse about the journey of rising up, I'm going to keep this little small group guide simple.

It is my vision that groups of women all over the country, and the world, will gather together to spur each other on to RISE UP! with every part of their lives and make Jesus famous. As we've talked about all throughout this book, our journey won't be simple. But if you've been inspired by this book and decided to change, why do it by yourself? A group banded together out of love for Jesus and desire to do life differently holds much power in accountability and makes the journey more effective. Following are just a few helpful hints that I've discovered in my years of leading small group Bible studies.

It is my hope that your group will learn to trust each other and cultivate an atmosphere of authenticity among you. This does start with the leader though, so prayerfully consider how you personally add to the culture of authenticity with your group. Please don't feel that you need to know all the answers. It is okay to say, "I don't know, but I will look into it." If one of your girls brings up a difficult topic that you don't know how to respond to, continue the conversation to garner the opinions of others in the group. Then, I suggest talking to your pastor or women's ministry leader to get his or her thoughts. No one looks down on someone who admits she doesn't know. In fact, your group will see you as a woman who cares about getting to the truth if you commit to finding out an answer and reporting back at the next group meeting. The important thing is that you all prayerfully come before your King, get to a deep discussion based on Scripture, and look to each other for thoughts and feelings.

HELPFUL HINTS

- Wherever you decide to hold your conversation group, set it up with comfortable couches, chairs and pillows. This is easy to do at a house but takes a bit more intention if you are meeting at a church.
- Keep the group to no more than ten women. This helps the flow of conversation so everyone feels that they have a voice and are not lost in a big group.
- Don't feel as though you need to have a fancy food setup. I've spent hours preparing snacks for my girls, and they end up in Tupperware in my fridge—not eaten. Simple coffee, sodas, and water are really the maximum you need to set out.
- Though you want to keep the group free flowing and structured lightly, set a specific start and finish time for each meeting in order to be respectful of everyone's time.
- Collect the email addresses and phone numbers of everyone that signs up. Then, the day of your group, send out an email and text message to your members as a friendly reminder. You might feel like this is over doing it, but everyone likes to be reminded during her busy days.
- A great way to handle prayer requests and allow the women to engage with each other is to hand out index cards and have each participant write down one prayer request, her name, her e-mail address, and her phone number. Then put the cards in a pile, asking everyone to pick one random card. Ask each participant to touch base with the person on her card during the week, offering encouragement and prayer.

- Encourage your group to do the journal questions for each chapter. I purposefully didn't call these sections "homework," but these journals solidify the concepts in each chapter and are crucial to growth and engagement with the Lord. In addition to the RISE UP! conversation questions that follow, these journal questions can offer starting points for in-depth discussions. (Be sure not to discourage those who do not complete their journals, though.)

The idea of this *Just RISE UP!* Conversation Starter is to give you a launching off point for your discussions. I pray that this little guide will help you lead your friends in deep and meaningful conversations about the topics in this book. These days, we often find ourselves in surface-level conversations even when the discussion surrounds Bible topics. Use this as a guide and then ask your own follow-up questions to take the conversation to a deeper level. The following is a breakdown of each chapter, with one question from each section.

Chapter 1: A Life Of Praise

- What are your thoughts on the concept of living a life of praise? How do you define a life of praise?
- Take some time reading Psalm 145:1–7. What feelings of praise are conjured up in your heart and mind when reading David the psalmist's words? In light of our conversation about the phrase "Oh, my God!" how does this change your point of view in living a life of reverent praise?
- What do you see as the benefit of RISING UP and living a life of praise with your thoughts and words? How can this life of praise positively affect your thought life and then the words you express?
- Read the first paragraph under "Authentic Faith: Reverence and Commitment." What are your thoughts on the concept of outward

and inward reverence and commitment? How does Philippians 4:8–9 play into the concept of inward reverence?

- What is your definition of "doing life differently?" How are you encouraged and challenged to do life differently through your words, thoughts, and lifestyle?

Chapter 2: Be Kingdom Minded

- Read Psalm 145:10–11, 13. What challenges do you face (or might you anticipate) in living with a kingdom perspective? (Example: People might not "get" you or may think you are weird.)
- What are your thoughts on Hebrews 10:10 and the idea that we are made holy through Jesus? How does this affect your thoughts about rising up and making Jesus famous? Does it take some of the pressure off because you don't have to do this in your own strength?
- As a group, read out loud Matthew 7:24–29. What are some examples of times when the "storm" came and threatened your belief system or how you feel about God? Do you see the value of building your faith and your life on the firm foundation of God's kingdom? If so, how? If not, share your doubts.
- Flip to Journal 4 on page 153 and talk about various areas in your life where you all can truly love God with all your heart, soul, mind, and strength.
- How does this chapter challenge you to do life differently as you RISE UP! to make Jesus famous?

Chapter 3: Bow Low Before You RISE UP!

- Take a few minutes to read through Psalm 145 as a group. How is this scripture becoming more and more meaningful to you as we study it together?
- What comes to your mind when you read the words humble and humility? Is it negative or positive? Read Ephesians 3:16–19 as a group. What is your initial reaction to the idea of experiencing God's fullness and fulfillment in life as we bow low and bask in His love?
- Touch base with the group on their experience of prayer journaling in Journal 3.
- Read Psalm 145:8–9. How does this verse speak to you about the free gift of grace, mercy, and forgiveness of sins? Do you have a hard time accepting this gift? If so, why?
- How does this chapter challenge you to do life differently as you RISE UP! to make Jesus famous?

Chapter 4: Our Dreams, Purpose, and God's Agenda

- Read aloud my words from the beginning of the introduction: "The key is to allow God to do big things in our lives by seeking after Him instead of just seeking after a dream or a passion. Dreams and passions are good, but they are most effective if God is the one who plants and nurtures them in our lives." What are your thoughts on this?
- Read aloud Psalm 145:16 and Psalm 37:3–4. Do you think our desires and passions and dreams will transform and evolve when we delight in the Lord and wait expectantly? If so, how? Why do you think this is key in rising up to make Jesus famous?

- Discuss the concepts of flat motivational phrases we often find and use as Christians (found in section 3). Do you see the importance of leaning on the power and strength, love and direction that comes from God instead of a self-focused or lofty dream? (See 2 Timothy 1:4.)
- Discuss the concepts of restoration and revival in Journal 4. In which areas of your life do you need both restoration and revival?
- How has this chapter changed the way you look at dreams and purpose?

Chapter 5: RISE UP! with Influence

- Share your various spheres of influence and the challenges you may find in rising up and making Jesus famous within those spheres.
- Read as a group Matthew 7:13–14. Now, read through as a group the definition of the narrow road in section 2, "Influence on the Narrow Road." Discuss this concept as a group.
- Read James 1:2–4. How did you paraphrase this passage in Journal 3? What would you say to the notion that laying down our nets is something we work on—by the power of the Holy Spirit—on a daily basis? Does it encourage you or discourage you based on this scripture? Why?
- Take some time to allow everyone to share from the Conversation Conclusion. Pick a chapter that challenged you the most and share how you are prayerfully rising up in this area.

Thank you from the bottom of my heart for taking initiative to gather your friends and encourage them along their own RISE UP! journey. It is not easy to be a leader, but know that you are making an impact with your obedience to God as you lead this group. Here is my prayer for you, my friend . . .

Father God, I know that You are smiling right now as You look upon my friend's personal journey of rising up to make Your name famous. Keep her in Your perfect strength as she leads her friends in conversation and Bible study. Give her everything she needs to lean on You and Your perfect Scripture. We will give You the glory, Lord! Amen!

Acknowledgments

Greg ■ Grayson ■ Iris ■ Bebb ■ Hannah ■ Frank ■ Alee ■ Maleah ■ Kate ■ Jennifer K ■ Bethany ■ Jenifer J ■ Ashley ■ Wendy ■ Donna ■ Heather ■ Amanda ■ Brett ■ Rachel ■ Julie ■ Chelsey ■ Ryan ■ Tonya ■ Harmony ■ Ally ■ Julia ■ Jennifer B ■ Robin ■ Renee

A Bit About LIVE IT OUT! Ministries

LIVE IT OUT! is the ministry of Sarah Francis Martin. While it is a space online, LIVE IT OUT! is to Sarah a place where her readers can get real, raw and relevant while studying the Bible. Sarah has a passion to encourage women to live out the Kingship of Christ. She does just that via her writing, blogging, and speaking ministry. Both online and offline, Sarah enjoys mentoring as well as playing the role of the "friend next door" as she invites readers to grab their favorite hot beverage and their Bible while engaging with each other to see Jesus as King over every square inch of their lives. For more information about Sarah Francis Martin or to contact her for a retreat or women's event, visit www.liveitoutblog.com.

Notes

Introduction

1. If you can't name ways that the Lord is moving around you, it's okay. Take a few moments to ask God to open your heart and mind to see what He is, in fact, doing around you and in you.

Chapter 1

1. A. W. Tozer, *The Pursuit of God*, ch. 7, http://www.worldinvisible.com/library/tozer/5f00.0888/5f00.0888.07.htm.
2. The Free Dictionary, s.v. "lifestyle," accessed April 22, 2014, http://www.thefreedictionary.com/lifestyle.

Chapter 4

1. Merriam-Webster Online, s.v. "righteous," accessed April 23, 2014, http://www.merriam-webster.com/dictionary/righteous.